Make the Trade

Make the Trade

Dave Cummings

A Kansas City entrepreneur takes on Wall Street

First Printing: December 2016 – First Edition

ISBN 978-0-9982998-0-8

Dave Cummings
1251 NW Briarcliff PKWY, STE 700
Kansas City, MO 64116

www.makethetradebook.com

To my family and my associates.

Contents

Preface

My Mom and Dad each wrote a book about growing up and the experiences that shaped their lives. They gave their books to our family as gifts.

Over the years, several people have urged me to write a book. I first started thinking about it in 2009, the year I turned 40. I wrote an outline, even drafted a few pages, and then I got distracted and pushed the project to the back burner. Every now and then, I would take out my draft and add a few words. I usually did not get too far before something more urgent demanded my attention. Once, I considered hiring a ghost writer or an editor to help me finish the project. However, I ultimately decided that this was my story and I wanted to tell it in my own words.

Writing an autobiography caused me to reflect upon my life. What was I trying to accomplish? What was important? Why would anyone want to read about me? It was not easy for me to write and many times I set this project aside. Yet it always bothered me that I did not complete my assignment. The hardest part was deciding what to leave out. There were so many interesting people and I knew there would not be space to include them all.

This year, 2016, a couple things happened that made me realize it was time to quit procrastinating and finish the job. First, BATS went public. Second, my daughter left for college. I finally carved out some time to finish my manuscript. So anyway, this is my story. I hope you enjoy reading it. More importantly, I hope you can learn something that helps you in your own journey.

With this book, I hope to show people that Wall Street and the markets are not as mysterious as they sometimes appear. Regular people, if they work hard enough, can figure out the game.

---Dave Cummings

Part One

Tradebot

1. Introduction

It has been an interesting journey. The last seventeen years of my life have been like living in a movie stuck on fast forward. In 1999, I started my first business, Tradebot Systems, with a $10,000 investment. By 2016, my firm had racked up over a billion dollars in net revenue from trading. We took on Wall Street and won.

We didn't stop there. We literally rebuilt the market from the ground up. In 2005, we started a new stock exchange called BATS. By trading volume, BATS became the second largest stock market in America, going public in 2016.

We took our profits and started investing in real-estate projects. Our investments built projects that helped shape our community. These projects created hundreds of private sector construction jobs.

Yes, I made money, but I also gave back. My wife and I quietly gave over a tenth of our income to charity. One group we supported gave out scholarships, and another helped feed kids. We've donated to several good groups, all working to make the world a better place.

We raised two kids in a quiet suburb of Kansas City. They attended the same public school system where my mom taught for twenty years.

I have lived the American dream as I understood it. Along the way, I tried to be thoughtful. I wrestled with the timeless issue of money. I learned to build businesses and manage people. I am an unapologetic American Capitalist.

There are many who hate the rich, the upper 1%. That is unfortunate. Most of us did not start rich. We learned from others. We worked hard. We built businesses. We played by the rules. We paid our taxes.

It is time to stop. To pause and catch my breath. To write down the thoughts that have been bouncing around in my head for seventeen years.

So Let's Chat

Imagine we are sitting down for coffee in my office. Anyone who knows me knows I am not a formal person. Most days I wear a golf shirt, cargo shorts, and Nike tennis shoes to work. I hope you are not expecting a formal report, rather this book is intended as more of a fireside chat. I will probably ramble off in random directions, but I promise there are a few nuggets of wisdom somewhere in these pages.

I wrote this book the way I wanted to write this book, without hiring an editor, and without feeling the need to follow all the normal conventions. This book reads the way I speak. I'd rather be 'authentic' than 'polished'.

The heart of the story begins in chapter two. The remainder of this chapter describes my background and some of the elements that prepared me for my journey.

When my kids were little, I would often tuck them in at night and ask, "What was the best part of your day?" Likewise, this book contains some of my best memories from the past seventeen years. As you reflect on life, there will be struggles and lessons learned, but I think it is more important to remember the highlights.

Emulate Success

People have asked me "What is the secret of your success?" Well, for one thing, I packed my brain with tons of good ideas. In college, I started reading biographies, self-help books, and books about business. For the next 20 years, I averaged reading a book a week. I did not agree with everything I read. Rather, I tried to take away small pieces of wisdom from several sources. As I read the stories about successful people, I became more ambitious. 'Emulate Success' became one of my favorite sayings.

People have all kinds of hobbies. Mine is pondering businesses. Over the years, this odd addiction has led me to learn a little bit about an extremely wide range of topics.

Sitting at my computer with a large monitor and a high-speed internet connection, I often lose myself for hours googling topics. I am obsessive compulsive. I lock onto an idea and just cannot stop thinking about it for hours and sometimes days. My mind goes off on many tangents. Sometimes, this allows me to connect the dots in ways that other people do not see. Sometimes, it just makes me oddly annoying.

Family

I had a fairly typical middle-class upbringing in Kansas City. My dad began his career teaching math at North Kansas City High School. I was born in 1969. Eight months before I was born, my dad was hired by TWA and continued to work there for the next 30 years. He was a mid-level manager who seemed to have a different project every few years to keep him busy. Mom was a teacher. After taking 10 years off when my sister and I were little, Mom went back to teaching at a local elementary school.

When I was in junior high, my dad and two TWA associates started a small storefront business, CompuTeacher, with the goal of teaching people how to use personal computers. The business did not last long, but I learned a lot working there with my dad before I was old enough to get a real job.

My dad's side of the family is mostly Scottish. My mom's side is mostly German. The Scottish are known for great business minds like Adam Smith and Andrew Carnegie. The Germans are known for great engineering. My success in life has stemmed from my ability to combine business and engineering.

My dad grew up on a farm in Iowa with three brothers. My mom grew up on a farm in northern Missouri with two sisters. Our forefathers on both sides came to America in the 1800s. It was probably the opportunity to get cheap farmland that caused our ancestors to move to the Midwest instead of staying on the East Coast. Religion-wise, my parents and grandparents were all Methodist.

My parents were both of the first generation in their family to go to college. They met at Northwest Missouri State and were married shortly after they graduated. Both hold Master's degrees. Since I have only an undergraduate degree, my dad once joked that I was the one in the family that was the least educated.

7

Both of my parents believed strongly in education. They instilled in me a sense that my life was important, that I was put on this earth for some purpose.

Grandma and Grandpa Sager

"Hello, hello." This was Grandpa August Sager's greeting. Grandpa and Grandma led a simple life. They never had much money, but they were almost always happy. Grandpa was from a large family and was the oldest boy. He dropped out of school at an early age to help support his younger brothers and sisters. Sager Brothers' Garage sat on the edge of his 40 acre farm along Highway 169 in Stanberry, Missouri. They started out fixing Model Ts and Ford tractors. In the 1930s, Grandpa was struck with polio and from then on his legs did not work very well. However, he was determined to earn his own living and never take handouts. He designed custom braces for both legs with special sliding mechanisms that locked his knees straight when he stood up. With his braces, he could walk instead of being confined. I always thought of Grandpa as the original entrepreneur in our family.

Grandma Hellen Sager taught us to be nice to everyone you meet. She said you should live your life morally like it was on the front page of the paper, because someday it might be. During a couple of summers, my sister and I spent a week at our grandparent's farm. Our cousins lived close by and we had tons of fun.

Every summer, Grandma and Grandpa ran a fireworks stand. It was a chance for everyone in Stanberry to drop by and say 'Hi.' They used the money raised from the stand to take all of their grandkids to Worlds of Fun, the amusement park in Kansas City.

Grandma died when I was in college. At my wedding, Grandpa shared the key to his happy marriage. He said from this day forth, whenever your wife asks a question, the right answer is always, "Yes, dear."

Platte Woods Methodist

I have belonged to Platte Woods United Methodist Church my whole life. As I was growing up, our family went to church every Sunday, unless we were traveling. It was important for me to see my kids grow up in the same church as I did.

In 1970, my parents and some other couples started an adult Sunday school class called the Seekers. Forty-six years later, many of the same couples still meet every Sunday. They are most of my parents' best friends. They still travel and do stuff together. Over the years I have gotten to know many of my parents' friends. Most have kids about my age. Several were my Sunday school teachers growing up. The lessons I learned in Sunday school influence my business instincts today. When my family attends worship service on Sundays, we are often greeted at the door by the Seekers.

Boy Scout Troop 314 met at the church. I was in the program for five years. We went camping each month, including ten-day summer sessions at the H. Roe Bartle Scout reservation in Osceola, Missouri. I just thought we were having fun and did not realize how much we were learning on our campouts. Learning often happens when you get outside your comfort zone. I became an Eagle Scout 32 years ago.

Chess, Monopoly, and Risk

Jeff Fink was my childhood best friend. We met in Miss Jones' third grade reading class. Probably to keep us from causing trouble, Miss Jones let Jeff and I play chess in class if we finished our assignment early. I learned to read very quickly so that I'd have more time to play chess.

Jeff was very smart. We were evenly matched and we were very competitive. After school, I would bike over to his house and we would play board games. Our three favorite games were Chess, Monopoly, and Risk.

Chess is a game of strategy. There is no luck. To win, it helps if you can see more moves ahead than your opponent.

Monopoly is a game about real estate and trading. You often have to give up one property in order to trade for another and make a monopoly. Once you get a monopoly, the key question is how much do you want to risk building houses and hotels? There is always the risk of bankruptcy.

Risk is a game about conquering the world. There is a lot of strategy in choosing when and where to attack. If you expand too quickly, you leave yourself too thin and are likely to lose when you are inevitably counter-attacked.

Chess, Monopoly, and Risk. I got very good at all three games. Not world-class competitive, but competitive enough to usually beat anyone else in our school, except Jeff. I spent hours growing up with these games. The lessons I learned were priceless.

Trading Baseball Cards

The Kansas City Royals were an exciting baseball team when I was growing up. Always the underdogs against the Yankees, they had young stars like George Brett. There was a ten year span where they made the playoffs six times: 1976, 1977, 1978, 1980, 1982, and 1985.

In 1978, Jeff Fink got me into baseball cards by selling me ten cards for a dime. Most boys collected cards. None of us had much money so we traded with each other all the time. I realized I could make money trading cards. My strategy was to trade kids the stars they wanted in exchange for their unloved cards. I got on the mailing list of a few baseball card dealers, and used their price list as a rough price guide. I memorized all the cards and what each was worth.

Little by little, I traded around the neighborhood and my collection grew. Except for my favorite George Brett rookie card, everything else in my collection was available for trade. I took money from birthday gifts and bought more packs of cards.

My cousins in Iowa were Cubs fans, so I took my cards up to family reunions and traded my Cubs cards for the Royals cards that were more valuable in KC. So today, I jokingly tell my Wall Street friends, "I was doing cross-market arbitrage by age ten."

In junior high I realized you could buy a wholesale case of 12,000 cards, sort them out, and make money trading or selling them to others. In 1985, I bought, sorted, and sold five cases containing 60,000 cards. The Royals won the World Series in 1985. Then they totally sucked for 28 years and did not make the playoffs.

I still have many of my old baseball cards. My favorite George Brett rookie card sits in my office.

Sports

Sports taught me some important lessons about life.

My eighth grade P.E. class had a four-week wrestling segment. At the end, we had a mini-tournament in class. I won my weight class. Coach Columbus encouraged me to go out for the school team, so I did. My eighth grade year, our team was horrible and went 0-6.

Coach Ballard was the girls' gymnastic coach, winning several state championships. He started talking smack to Coach Columbus and somehow dropped gymnastics and became the wresting coach for my ninth grade year. He focused on recruiting the best athletes for his team.

"Success belongs to those who believe in succeeding," Coach Ballard repeated over and over as we lifted weights. He pushed us hard. Leadership matters. We were undefeated that year going 6-0. I learned an important lesson – recruiting the best talent is the fastest way to improve your team.

In high school, I ran cross country and track for Coach Potter. Cross country starts with disciplined training. To prepare for the season, each morning I would run 5.25 hilly miles around Weatherby Lake with my teammate and neighbor Bobby Renton. Cross country is also about pushing through the pain. I'm not too into putting myself through pain, so I was never very good.

I was an average athlete but not anywhere close to the best. My mind was competitive, but my body just could not deliver. Without the regular thrill of victory, I lost interest in sports.

Engineering

Legos were my favorite toy. I wonder how many future engineers grew up playing with Legos. I also had Tinker Toys, Lincoln Logs, and model trains.

Dad bought me my first computer in 1982. It was a TRS-80 Color Computer. It originally had 4k of memory, which we upgraded to 32k. At age 13, I taught myself how to program using Microsoft Basic.

In 1984, Dad upgraded me to an IBM PCjr. It had 128k of memory and a 3 ½ inch floppy drive. Computers were getting more powerful every year. For my birthday, I got a computer chess program. It was fun to play, but the computer was not very good. I quickly learned to beat the program.

My early interest in computers led me to pursue a career in software development. I got my undergraduate degree in Computer and Electrical Engineering from Purdue University. Like many computer enthusiasts, I was rather introverted and often socially awkward.

During college, I was in an internship program with Eastman Kodak and spent three semesters working in Rochester, New York. My co-workers and I ventured up to Toronto several times. I liked visiting Canada.

General Motors

I spent my last summer in college interning at General Motors in Anderson, Indiana. After graduation, I went to work as a plant engineer in their battery factory in Olathe, Kansas. Manufacturing was interesting to me. Understanding the proper role of unions and management was a good learning experience. The guys on the line treated me well and were happy to explain what they did. The one overall theme, though, was 'never rock the boat'. The old timers told me GM was a bureaucracy that moved at a certain pace and I needed to learn to accept it rather than try to swim upstream. I enjoyed my job at GM, but after about six months I realized I could get ahead much faster in a smaller organization, so I quit.

Wall Street

I always had a fascination with the stock market. The great crash of 1987 happened my first semester in college. That day, I started reading the *Wall Street Journal*, a practice I have continued most mornings since.

Every Friday night, PBS carried a show called *Wall Street Week with Louis Rukeyser*. I loved that show. The panelists explained the market and which stocks they liked. When the market sold off, Louis Rukeyser told people not to panic. He was always optimistic about the long run.

My senior year in college, I got cable television for the first time. CNBC was a channel that covered the market all day, every day. There was something exciting about watching Maria Bartiromo and Bob Pisani report live from the floor of the New York Stock Exchange. I became more and more interested in the market.

Charles Schwab

The Berlin Wall fell in 1989. I watched images of people partying in Germany as they ripped down pieces of the wall. The Cold War was over. The commentators pondered the implications of world peace.

In June 1990, I opened a stock account with Charles Schwab with some money saved from my internships. Defense contractors were trading at ridiculously low price-earnings ratios. My first trade was buying 100 shares of General Dynamics (the maker of the F-16) at $30. On August 2nd, Iraq invaded Kuwait. Defense stocks soared. It was like free money. I was hooked on trading.

Over the next five years, I saved what money I could and added it to my account. I traded in and out of positions. Some trades made money and some trades lost. I hated losing. I turned to technical analysis, hoping to find a system that would increase my odds.

Cerner

After a brief stint with a computer consulting company, I joined Cerner Corporation, the industry leader in healthcare information software. Neal Patterson is the CEO. When I started, the company had about 500 people (in 2016 it has about 22,000). Cerner was a very entrepreneurial place. It was growing so fast that it always seemed to be on the edge of chaos. In my three years there, I had six different managers. Neal insisted on calling us 'associates' instead of 'employees', a practice I later copied at Tradebot. He held a company-wide town hall meeting once a quarter where he laid out the company's vision.

If you aspire to someday start your own business, go to work for a successful entrepreneur. The lessons I learned at Cerner were far more valuable than my paycheck. I was at Cerner for three years, from 1992 to 1995.

Jamie

In 1993, my friend Scott Fitzgerald invited me to visit a dog-track called the Woodlands. He introduced me to a handful of his friends, including Jamie Troyer. Jamie and I started dating later that year.

As we dated, we talked about our life goals. I told her I wanted to have a boy and a girl and joked they should both be born on a Saturday. I told her I wanted to start my own business someday. She said something that became a running joke in our house, "Ok, be as successful as you want, as long as you are home for dinner by six o'clock!" We got engaged the night before Thanksgiving and were married in April 1994.

Jamie was a surety underwriter with Fireman's Fund. She bonded several highway and building contractors in the area including Clarkson Construction and Garney Construction. When she walked a job site, she would point out the little things. A number of little things wrong indicate a poorly managed business. She was trained to assess the risk that a business would fail.

Growing up in Eastern Colorado, Jamie never had much money, but to her credit, family was always much more important to Jamie than money. She was raised to be strictly honest. Jamie is also fiercely loyal. She is always there for her family and friends in good times and bad.

The Worst Stockbroker

After getting married, I thought I wanted to be a stockbroker. I interviewed for a job with a big Wall Street firm. Shortly into the conversation, the manager stared at me and said in a serious voice,

"Son, you'd be the worst stockbroker in the world."

He explained that his business was all about sales and had nothing to do with picking stocks. My heart sank. Then, he pointed out his window at the Kansas City Board of Trade (KCBT), "That's like a big poker game. You belong over there, kid."

Kansas City Board of Trade

At first, my wife was not too keen about my new passion. After much debate, she agreed to let me quit my job at Cerner and lease a seat at the KCBT for six months. "Get it out of your system before we have kids," she said. We could live on her salary for a while if we had to. Well, I found a way to make more in those six months than I did in my previous year of programming. So Jamie let me stay for what became three years. I eventually bought a seat and traded wheat, wheat options, and Value Line stock index futures in the pits.

I would not want to go back to pit trading, but I am so thankful that I had the experience. The pits are a nasty place to earn a living. All day long you are face to face with screaming traders and brokers. You are trying to take their money, and they are trying to take yours. It is physical. It is intense. Mistakes cost money. A thick skin is required. You control your emotions. You control your risk. Once a pit trader, you are always a pit trader. It is difficult to convey the experience to someone who has never traded in a commodities pit. On one level, you hate everyone around you, but on another level, there is a deep sense of respect.

In the pits, 'palms in' means you are buying, and 'palms out' means you are selling. When the big guys' palms were in, my reflexes put my palms in without thinking. I watched the floor with one eye and the quote boards with the other. An uptick in corn caused me to buy wheat. I quickly learned how to make money trading in the pits.

I was not there to make friends. I was there to make money. At 25, I was younger than most at the KCBT. I played strictly by the rules, but I was ruthlessly aggressive. My first week in the wheat pit, Mike Adams, one of the longtime ringleaders, joked, "Cummings, you are the third most hated guy in this pit, and the other two guys took twenty years to develop their reputations." I took that as I sign that I must be doing something right. I was not there to make friends. I was there to make money.

Nicole

Our daughter Nicole has an extremely strong personality. Born in 1997, she was literally kicked out of the hospital nursery hours after being born because she was crying loudly and keeping the other babies awake. Jamie was exhausted. I stayed up all night holding Nicole on my chest, her first night in this world, rubbing her back. When she could hear my heartbeat, she fell asleep.

As she was growing up, Nicole often joined me when I was watching the CBS Evening News or The O'Reilly Factor. She also liked business shows on CNBC like 'The Profit' and 'Shark Tank'. When she did not understand something, she made me pause the TiVo and explain it to her. We frequently paused to debate and discuss the issues of the day. Over the years, many people have commented that Nicole thinks about issues like an adult. Well, eighteen years of debating with me will do that to a person.

Nicole has a strong sense of fashion and taste. She always dresses extremely well. I, on the other hand, could not care less about what brands I wear. Even after I became a millionaire, I still bought most of my clothes at Kohl's because it was cheap. This was embarrassing to Nicole. One time she implored, "Daddy, I won't ask you to shop at Neiman Marcus, but can you at least promise me you will try Dillard's? You are banned from Kohl's." So, we went to Dillard's and she picked me out a whole new wardrobe of polo shirts. I nearly died paying over $70 for each shirt, knowing I could get perfectly fine Croft and Barrow shirts at Kohl's for $10. These days I mostly shop at Dillard's, but occasionally I will sneak back into Kohl's when Nicole is not around.

After Nicole was born, Jamie gave up her career to stay home. Though she has never had a formal role, Jamie and I frequently talk about my businesses. Over the years, she's become a very trusted advisor. On many occasions, she's helped me think through a difficult issue or reduce the risk in a situation.

Electronic Trading

By 1998, electronic trading was sweeping Europe. Some of the markets in Europe switched almost overnight from the pits to electronic trading. In America, the conversion took much longer than most people predicted. The Chicago Mercantile Exchange (CME) launched the Globex platform in 1992. By 1998, it was just starting to gain significant volume. Ten years after the Globex launch, there were still some major products traded in the pits in Chicago.

Kasparov vs Deep Blue

One day, an idea came to me that would change the course of my life. I read in the Wall Street Journal that Gary Kasparov, the world chess champion, was defeated by a computer program from IBM called Deep Blue. I pondered the implications of this classic man vs machine struggle.

> *"If computers could be programmed to beat Kasparov, then maybe computers could be programmed to beat the market..."*

2. Spare Bedroom

A Globex terminal from the Chicago Mercantile Exchange arrived at my house in January of 1999. It was an ordinary Windows-based personal computer with special software loaded on it by the exchange to allow futures trading.

My wife and I lived in a typical story-and-a-half house at the end of a quiet cul-de-sac in a northern suburb of Kansas City. Our one-year-old daughter, Nicole, slept in the middle bedroom on the second floor. At the end of the hallway was a spare bedroom where I set up my home office. It wasn't too fancy, just three cheap fake wood desks along the outer walls with a closet on the remaining side. Two hand-made wooden bookcases, built by my great uncle Walt, held my growing collection of books.

I set up my Globex terminal on the north-facing desk. The south-facing desk held my other computer, which I used for programming. The middle desk by the window held a phone and my paperwork. We had to get a dedicated T1 line in order to support the Globex terminal. The data line literally ran down the side of our house and through the back yard. That summer, I had to be extra careful when mowing our yard not to cut the line and ruin my business.

There was a window which looked over the driveway of the house next to ours. I would occasionally see Nicole's babysitter, Katy Barth, playing basketball in the driveway with her friends. She was 12. One day, Katy asked me what I was working on up there.

Trading Robot
I told her my crazy idea was to build a "Trading Robot" that would trade like a pit trader, only much faster. Then, I would be able to trade many securities around the world at the same time, rather than standing in a single pit in Kansas City. Katy seemed interested, but most other people I shared the idea with thought it was nutty.

The rules of chess were simple and well defined. Stock trading was abstract. How could a computer program incorporate all of the subtleties of human traders? Why would you let a program risk real money? What if it got out of control?

"Tradebot" was the name I gave the business. It was short for "Trading Robot", similar to the way "Microsoft" was short for "Microcomputer Software." In the beginning, I envisioned Tradebot as a one-man operation, with me doing both the programming and the trading. There were no plans to hire others or expand outside my home office. I just wanted to make enough money to support my family.

"My original goal for Tradebot was to make $100,000 a year."

The year before, my wife had left her job so she could spend time with our baby daughter. We had no safety net. Failure was not an option. She gave me three months to make the new business profitable or I needed to go back to the pits.

Off the Ground

I think all good entrepreneurs are a little bit crazy. We tend to be unrealistically optimistic about our chance for success. Looking back, my business had every reason to fail. I was undercapitalized, trying an unproven business model, and I did not have any management experience. I was trying to do the whole thing without any help. I pulled several all-nighters. I programmed and traded at the same time. I have never worked so hard in my life. It was mentally exhausting.

There is nothing like a deadline. By March, the first version of my bot started making money. Not much money, but just enough to keep me going. My business has been profitable every month since.

The first Tradebot strategies were extremely simple. On the floor of the CME, they traded S&P 500 futures in the pit. On Globex, you could trade Mini S&P contracts that were one-fifth of the size of the regular contracts. At night, both contracts traded side-by-side on Globex. I realized you could price the Mini's based on the bigger contracts and make a few hundred dollars a week. Other early strategies like legging into calendar spreads were also very simple.

Dan & Steve

My bots were starting to make some money, but most of the money I made was paid in commissions to my broker. In order to make more money, I needed to find a cheaper broker. I picked up *Futures Magazine* and started calling brokers looking around for a better rate. Upon hearing about my small account size, most of the big-name brokers did not seem too interested in letting me open an account.

One call was different. A half-page advertisement showed a pit broker standing in front of a bank of twelve computer monitors. It caught my attention. I gave the number a call. Dan Tierney answered. I told him about my idea for 'Trading Robots'. He seemed interested. He told me he was partners with Steve Schuler. Steve was the guy pictured in the ad in his pit trading jacket. Dan suggested I visit the two of them in Chicago.

I bought a cheap ticket on Southwest, landed at Midway, and took the Orange Line downtown. Steve was a broker in the S&P pit. Dan and three other guys were jam-packed in a 12' by 12' office in the CME Building at 30 South Wacker. They had tons of computers everywhere including the bank of monitors that I saw in the ad. Networking wires and power cords ran every which way across the floor.

Dan, Steve, and a couple other partners ran a business called Excel Systems. Dan had spent countless hours finding and researching futures trading systems that they could license from the authors and charge customers a commission to use. It was a good idea in theory, but in practice, the trading systems would quit working and the customers would lose money and close their accounts.

From our first conversation, Dan asked tons of great questions, and seemed to intuitively get the concept that computers could be used for short-term pit-style trading. Steve may have been a bit more skeptical but saw Dan's excitement and decided "why not give it a try." They let me open an account and gave me an ultra-cheap rate that made my trading system more profitable. Week after week, my account balance started to climb.

Dan kept calling me to share ideas and ask questions. He was an

21

encyclopedia of trading ideas. Dan was eager to find a programmer so he could try his trading ideas in the market. In July 1999, we worked out a consulting agreement where they paid me $5,000 a month. I agreed to spend one week a month in Chicago programming Dan's ideas, and they got to use a copy of my software for their own trading. Our consulting arrangement lasted three months.

Chicago

Imagine playing little league ball and then stepping up to the plate at Wrigley field – that's how I felt. In comparison to Kansas City, trading in Chicago was done on a massive scale. Before 9/11, the CME and the Chicago Board of Trade (CBOT) both had visitor galleries that were open to the public. One day, I just stood in the visitor gallery for two hours mesmerized by all the action on the trading floor. I bought a necktie in the gift shop. It featured a cartoon showing a bunch of pit traders waving their arms. My business regularly takes me to New York where I have to wear a suit and tie, which I hate. I often wear my traders tie to mock the formality of New York City and remind people that I started in the pits.

While consulting for Dan and Steve, I stayed at the Blackstone Hotel. In those days, it was pretty run down. I didn't care. It was the cheapest hotel within walking distance of the exchanges. At night, I would often take long wandering walks around the loop, down to Shedd Aquarium, and over to Navy Pier. I pondered trading strategies and the bigness of Chicago.

During the main part of the day, I programmed in Dan and Steve's office. After the market closed, Dan and I would often go out for pizza and discuss trading theories. One analogy he shared was to imagine all markets worldwide connected by invisible rubber bands. Related assets could move around a bit, but if they moved far enough, they exerted a force on similar assets trading in other markets. Most of the successful models we built were based around trading something relative to the price of related markets. Dan always took a global view of trading. He believed that the price of every asset was related to the price of every other asset.

Family Trip One

I frequently talk about my business with my family. I wanted them to see the markets firsthand and meet some of the people that I knew. Over the next seventeen years, I took a series of five 'family trips' with members of my family, in addition to our normal family vacations.

Family trip one was to Chicago. After a week of consulting with Dan and Steve in Chicago, I was joined for a few days by Jamie and Nicole. Nicole was almost two, and Jamie was pregnant with our second child. I took them down to the visitors' gallery. Next, I introduced them to Dan and Steve. We took a Wendella boat ride down the Chicago River and out onto Lake Michigan. We had fun looking around the city. Nicole liked the penguins at Shedd Aquarium.

However, I made one mistake. We stayed at the Blackstone. Jamie pointed out that it was dirty and the shower was cold. She was not too happy with my hotel selection. She banned me from ever staying at the Blackstone again.

Getco

Tradebot was originally intended to be a one man operation. Dan and Steve encouraged me to keep raising the bar. "If you have a winning trade, you need to press it," Dan would say. They convinced me that maybe a real business with employees could be created around my "Trading Robots".

In October 1999, Dan and Steve started Getco. Getco stood for "Global Electronic Trading Company". Steve proposed we combine forces and each own a third of the company. I turned down his offer. With both of them in Chicago and me in KC, I did not want to be the odd man out. Instead, I decided to start a separate business in Kansas City.

Getco had access to capital. I always admired Dan and Steve and what they built. They were a very positive force in the industry. Getting ahead of my story a bit, Getco grew at an incredible pace. By 2007, Getco had become the largest player worldwide in high-frequency trading and was enormously profitable. Dan once told me he wanted to grow Getco, "into the next Goldman Sachs".

23

A few people have suggested I made a huge mistake turning down one-third equity in Getco. I disagree. Running my own business turned out to be the right decision for me. Yet, I often looked up to Getco, as a beacon of what was possible in the trading industry.

The Economist & The Trader

In 1999, Dan told me a joke which epitomizes our business:

> *"One day a famous economist and a trader are walking down LaSalle Street in Chicago. They both see what appears to be a $20 bill lying on the sidewalk. The economist argues that is impossible. The sidewalk approximates an efficient market. Thousands of people pass by daily, so someone would have instantaneously corrected any possible inefficiency. There is no way a $20 bill could be just lying in the street. The trader nods in agreement. The two men change the subject and keep walking. As they pass by the bill, the trader quietly bends down and puts the twenty in his pocket."*

In top business schools, they teach the Efficient Market Hypothesis:

> *"In finance, the efficient market hypothesis (EMH), or the joint hypothesis problem, asserts that financial markets are 'informationally efficient'. In consequence of this, one cannot consistently achieve returns in excess of average market returns on a risk adjusted basis, given the information available at the time the investment is made."* – Wikipedia

Eugene Fama of the University of Chicago is the father of the efficient market hypothesis. In 2013, he won the Nobel Prize in Economics. What? Have the eggheads in the ivory towers never heard of Getco or Tradebot? When I read he won, it reminded me of the joke above. In his prize-winning theory, we do not exist.

I will never win a Nobel Prize. I am not welcome in the ivory tower. My place in this world is to quietly pick up $20 bills.

Software License

Getco agreed to license Tradebot software and trading models in exchange for 25% of the trading profits they made with our software. They even agreed to pre-pay some of the money so I could hire more programmers and expand. It was a non-exclusive deal, so we could also license the models to others or trade the models ourselves if we wanted.

I thought about which programmers I wanted to work with to expand my business. Tom Armstrong was at the top of my list. For a while, he was my team leader at Cerner before he left to work at DST. Being a couple years older than me, he was a good mentor. Tom placed a strong emphasis on proper software design techniques. He had written four books about programming. It was hard to convince Tom to leave the security of DST for an upstart like Tradebot, but we desperately needed a great software developer.

Getting Incorporated
Before I could expand my business and hire employees, I needed to get properly organized and incorporated.

Keith Milburn is a friend of my parents from church who ran his own warehousing business. My dad suggested I speak to Keith about starting my business. Keith introduced me to an attorney named Craig Salvay.

Craig is about 15 years older than me. He is very polished and a deep thinker. We met over pizza at Stone Canyon in Parkville. Over time, he has become a mentor and a respected friend. Craig helped me with the legal aspects of incorporating, setting up a board of directors, and dealing with shareholders.

Tradebot Launch
Tradebot Systems, Inc. was incorporated on October 12, 1999.

"My investment in Tradebot was $10,000."

I bought ten million shares at a tenth of a cent per share apiece. For the same price per share, small amounts of shares were also sold to Dan and Steve at Getco, Tom Armstrong, Craig Salvay, and my father.

Steve Schuler, Craig Salvay, and I formed our initial board of directors. I took the title of CEO and Chairman of the Board.

The first six months, Tradebot had just three employees. Tom and I did the programming and Dad did everything else, from finance to office space to stocking the company with drinks.

There is something special about a business that spans multiple generations. It was great to once again work with my dad. As a teenager, I had once worked in his business, Compu-Teacher. Now the roles were reversed and he was working for my company. His experience helped us get started on the right track and I am very thankful for that.

How Much is Enough?

I just wanted to get incorporated quick and easy, but Craig wanted to analyze everything and make sure it was set up properly. In our early conversations, he had one question he just would not let go of:

"Dave, how much is enough?"

I replied, "I don't know. You just keep raising the bar." He said he knew some very rich people who were miserable chasing after money. "How much is enough?" he kept asking me despite my repeated attempts to dodge the question. He was not going to let me incorporate until I answered the question, "How much is enough?" Finally, in exasperation, I blurted out, "Ten million dollars!" At the time, it was more than a hundred times my net worth. "Promise me one thing, Dave", Craig's voice lowered to a deep baritone,

"If you get your $10 million, remember to be happy!"

3. Armour & Erie

After getting incorporated, Tradebot needed office space. Dad and I looked into renting space in a nice office tower near the airport. The building was owned by a big out-of-town real estate investment trust. The REIT required a ten year lease, and since Tradebot had no assets, they also demanded a personal guarantee. In my head, I multiplied 120 times the monthly rent. It was more than I was willing to risk. I was bummed.

By chance, Dad saw a small ad for office space in one of those free papers that get thrown in your driveway. We went and checked out the space at 320 Armour Road. It was an old concrete bank building from the 1920's that stood on the corner of Armour and Erie.

Downtown North Kansas City looked like Mayberry on the Andy Griffith show. It was an unlikely place to start a high-tech trading company. We joked that the center of the trading universe would one day be at the corner of Armour and Erie but nobody knew it yet.

Concerned Care

Concerned Care is a not-for-profit that owned the building and used the first floor. On the second floor were four suites of about a thousand square foot each that they rented out. The middle one was available.

As luck would have it, Karl Morris was a counselor at North Kansas City High School before he started Concerned Care. He and my dad just hit it off. He told us about his 26 year quest to setup family-like group homes for developmentally disabled adults, rather than letting them live in mental institutions. "Live in the world of possibility" was Karl's motto. We told Karl about the REIT and asked him for better terms. He told us he would give us a month-to-month lease if we would just "Live in the world of possibility". Compared to the REIT, it sounded like a great deal. We signed.

For the next nine years, Tradebot lived upstairs from Concerned Care.

Over time, we persuaded their other tenants to move out so we could expand into their space. At one point, Concerned Care even converted a conference room in the basement for us to use. In 2004, we punched a hole in a wall and expanded into an old print shop next door.

Robert was a developmentally challenged individual that worked the front desk for Concerned Care. Each day when I entered the building, Robert would wave and smile. I do not ever recall seeing Robert unhappy. Concerned Care helped him live his life to the fullest.

Every now and then, Karl came up to our offices to check on how the stock market was performing that day. He became another one of my mentors. I never forgot the break he cut us when we were starting out. As our resources grew, I donated a significant amount of money to Concerned Care. Karl was wise, and in the end he got a much higher return on his building than the arrogant out-of-town REIT.

When Karl retired in 2007, they established the "Karl Morris Legacy Award" to recognize friends of Concerned Care. At a gala fundraising banquet, Karl surprised me by announcing that I had won the award. To this day, it is one of my most prized possessions. I told the audience, "Tradebot just makes money. You change people's lives."

When I finished speaking, the band started playing. Robert was first to the dance floor with a girl who was also a Concerned Care resident. They danced. I was so happy for him. A tear ran down my cheek.

Small Mistakes

I made many small mistakes in the early days of Tradebot. I had never managed anything before. Dad tried hard to coach me. From time to time, he would invite me to lunch at Chappell's, the sports bar across the street. He would go over his list of everything he saw that I was doing wrong. It drove me nuts. But, I have to admit, he was usually right.

Dad taught me a technique he called "Management by wandering around." Each day since, I have tried to make a couple laps around our floor, stopping to chat with associates along the way or at the coffee pot. It is the best way I know to stay in touch with our team.

Small mistakes were fine. We just tried to "fail quickly", learn from the mistake and try something else.

Dot Com Era

Tradebot incorporated in October 1999, right at the peak of the dot-com bubble. In this era, many technology companies were raising tons of cash and burning through it to get big quickly. Getco pushed us to move faster. They wanted us to raise capital, hire more programmers, and expand quickly. Being a relatively new manager, I was reluctant at first.

In February 2000, I finally relented and started making plans to raise capital. Jamie was eight months pregnant with our second child. Craig Salvay helped me put together an offering memorandum. We sent it out to several institutional investors. Most never even called us back. Craig invited the head trader from American Century (a mutual fund company headquartered in Kansas City) to visit our offices. He remarked, "Looks interesting, but it will never scale." Looking back, I understand now why it was hard to raise 'professional money'. We were just too scrappy.

Rob Alumbaugh

In Tradebot's early days, our recruiting was done through word-of-mouth referrals from people we knew.

Rob was a friend of Tom Armstrong's who worked at DST. He was about my age. According to Tom, he was one of the best developers at DST. Rob had a Datek account and was day trading stocks as a hobby. I knew from our first conversation that Rob would be a perfect fit for Tradebot.

There was just one problem. Dot-com mania was raging, and we had not yet received any additional capital.

Biz Space, an online publishing company, had raised more than $10 million in funding and was also aggressively recruiting Rob. Our offer to Rob was $10,000 below Biz Space's. He turned us down and told us he had accepted the job at Biz Space.

I called my wife to share the disappointing news that we would not be able to hire Rob. Jamie said, "If he's really good, pay up and hire the best." I told her I had no idea how we could make payroll. "Don't worry about it. Get him," she said. This was one of the few times my wife was more optimistic than I was about the business. We called Rob back and raised his offer $20,000. He accepted.

Funding Round

In March 2000, about a month after we hired Rob, we closed our investment round, the same month that the Nasdaq stock market peaked at 5,132. Nice timing.

Tradebot raised $650,000 at a price per share of 37 cents. Getco invested $500,000. The remaining shares were bought by my uncle Chuck, my uncle Don, Don's friend Denny Nelson, Dad's friend and former TWA boss Arnie Grotenhuis, and Craig's attorney-friend Chuck Rouse.

There was an interesting condition on the Getco investment:

> ***Tradebot was now required to allow Getco access to <u>all</u> trading software and trading models that we produced.***

Getco continued to pay a licensing fee equal to 25% of the net trading profits they made with our software. The deal was still non-exclusive. In fact, our business plans called for eventually adding several more firms as licensees.

Tradebot also had the right to use our software internally to trade for our company account. Over time, we would come to realize that doing our own trading was more profitable than licensing our software to others.

From 1999 to 2001, the software license revenue from Getco was the majority of the revenue at Tradebot.

With our funding in place, we had a little more breathing room.

Joe

Our son Joe was born in April 2000. Joe has always been an easy going, generally happy child. Two years behind his sister in school, Joe and Nicole are closer than most siblings. Joe often likes to hang out with Nicole and her friends.

As our kids were growing up, I frequently discussed my business with them. I told the kids Tradebot was in the business of making money. One day, my wife and kids dropped by the office. Joe was about four. He stuck his tiny fingers in the disk drive hole on one of the computers. He looked up at me and asked, "Daddy is this where the money comes out?"

Your kids learn more than you realize sometimes. When Joe was about nine, I was taking him and his friend Tripp to soccer practice. Tripp was sore because his dad made him rake leaves all morning. Tripp said, "My dad is teaching me to work hard, so someday I will be able to get a job." My son shot back, "My dad is teaching me to hire people like you."

The thing I admire most about Joe is his ability to live in the moment. One day, I asked him his goals for the upcoming summer. He said, "Dad, I don't have goals. I just wake up each day and try to be happy. To find someone to hang out with or something fun to do."

Joe likes to build things. One summer he and his grandpa Rich built a treehouse together. For Christmas, he asked for the parts to build his own computer.

Joe and I are pretty close. Sometimes, he is like the brother I never had. We like to do fun things together like wakeboarding or riding ATV's. Last year, the two of us took a trip to Cedar Point to ride roller coasters.

Unlike me, both of my kids make friends easily wherever they go. Even on vacation, they meet people. They stay in touch with their new friends on social media, often for years after the trip. Both Nicole and Joe have a deep sense of right and wrong. Both are mature beyond their years. Both talk like adults. People tend to assume they are older than they really are.

God gave us one boy and one girl, both born on Saturday.

Kelly Burkhart

Kelly Burkhart was a developer I knew from my Cerner days. Kelly joined Tradebot in June 2000.

Kelly and I used to joke that the top 3% of the programmers did 50% of the real work, and that the bottom 80% of the programmers actually did 'negative work' when you included the cost of fixing their bugs. That was the thinking that led Tradebot to hire only the best of the best for our programming team. Kelly is a world-class C++ programmer and database architect. I was glad to add him to our team.

Tradebot Version Two
We began working on the second major version of the bot. The first version of the bot worked exclusively on CME Globex terminals. The second version of our product was based around an application programming interface (API) from Interactive Brokers (IB). Using the API made the code much faster and more reliable.

IB was one of the few brokers at the time that offered a computer interface or API. Having a computer interface was critical. There was not enough time to hand key in orders over the internet like you would with an account from Ameritrade or Schwab.

I split my time between programming, trading, and trying to be CEO. I personally wrote the part of the code that we called 'the bot'. It made the buying and selling decisions. Other parts of the code were designed and written by Tom Armstrong, Rob Alumbaugh, and Kelly Burkhart. Dad continued to do the accounting and anything else we needed.

Proprietary Trading
The term 'proprietary trading' means trading in the firm account rather than the account of a customer.

In summer 2000, Tradebot hired our first full-time trader and he began trading Tradebot's money. Little by little, as we got more capital, our focus shifted away from software licensing and into proprietary trading.

Our First Major Setback
Our small team of six was working hard. We had a lot of code to write and had no shortage of new ideas to try.

In September 2000, we suffered what I consider my first major setback. Biz Space hired Tom Armstrong away from us by offering him a good helping of stock options. It was a difficult blow because Tom was one of the co-founders and owned Tradebot stock with no vesting requirement. It really hurt my feelings when he left. He was the first associate to quit.

Upon reflection, I do not really blame Tom for leaving. The tech world is always at war for top talent. Biz Space was a cool dot com company and had over $10 million in funding. At Biz Space, he was able to manage a whole department of programmers.

Eighteen months later, Tradebot repurchased Tom's stock for $225,000. He had paid $300 for it. It was a pricey lesson. Yet, there was one silver-lining: I never would have met Rob Alumbaugh if it were not for Tom.

4. Stocks

In 2000, Tradebot's focus shifted from futures to stocks.

The first version of the bot traded only CME futures. The second version of the bot, with the API, also allowed us to trade stocks.

In order to explain our approach to stock trading, I first need to explain the market structure differences between futures trading and stock trading. I also need to explain some history about the markets. For those not familiar with the stock market industry, this may seem a bit technical, but please bear with me.

CME Monopoly

Futures exchanges and stock exchanges operate very differently. Each futures exchange, like the CME, has a monopoly on all the futures products that trade on its exchange. All the orders for a single product go to a single place.

By contrast, stocks trade on many markets at the same time. The markets are linked together electronically. Brokers route customer orders to the market which offers the best price. This competition between the stock markets is a very good thing for investors. It forces stock markets to innovate and compete for business. Competition between stock markets did not happen on its own. It was mandated by Congress with the Unlisted Trading Privileges Act of 1994. This act gives an exchange the right to trade a security that is not listed on their exchange.

There is no such rule in regards to futures trading. Having a monopoly on trading allows futures exchanges, like the CME, to charge relatively higher fees for matching buyers and sellers. In 2016, CME Group had a market capitalization of $35.7 billion. A monopoly is quite profitable if you are the one holding it, but it is not so great for your customers. The CME became a public company on December 5, 2002. Before that, it was owned by its members. When it was member owned, it ran as a not-for-profit co-operative and kept the trading fees as low as possible. Now that the CME is a for-profit public company, it is in their interest to charge as much as possible. The CME spends millions of dollars on lobbying in order to keep this powerful monopoly in place.

Anyway, let's now shift the focus to stock trading and stock market structure. It is not a perfect world, either.

New York Stock Exchange

The NYSE trading floor is the most visible symbol of American Capitalism at work. The image helps build investor confidence.

The New York Stock Exchange (NYSE) is the largest stock market in the world based on the market capitalization of its listed companies. Also called the Big Board, the NYSE traces its roots to the 1792 Buttonwood Agreement. This agreement set a minimum commission rate that its members could charge clients. It also required its members to give preference to other members instead of trading with non-members. From its very beginning, the NYSE was designed as a cartel.

In 1999, most of the trading on the NYSE was done on the trading floor. Each listed stock was assigned to a specialist post. The specialist was charged with maintaining a 'fair and orderly' market in their assigned stock. Floor brokers brought customer orders to the proper specialist post for trading. Orders could also be routed to the NYSE electronically using the DOT system, but most buy and sell orders would not match with each other until the specialist tapped on their keyboard.

When I started Tradebot in 1999, I remember looking at the NYSE website. NYSE proudly bragged, "We fill the average market order in only 23 seconds!" By contrast, the competing Nasdaq system could fill a market order in less than a second.

Before 2001, prices were quoted in fractions. The minimum increment was $1/16^{th}$ of a dollar ($0.0625), often called a 'teenie'.

The wider the spread between the bid and the offer, the more money the specialist could make by trading against the public. Spreads were often at least $1/8^{th}$, and frequently $1/4^{th}$ ($0.25). The entire system was designed to be as profitable as possible for the NYSE members. The

36

value of a NYSE 'seat' was over a million dollars. NYSE itself was a mutual company and operated for the benefit of its members. To put it bluntly, the old NYSE was a huge racket. Dick Grasso was its CEO. His main job was to protect the cartel.

Through an industry contact, I got a personal tour of the NYSE floor. We looked up at the famous balcony where the opening bell is rung. I caught a glimpse of Dick Grasso chatting with a floor broker. The history of the place was overwhelming. My tour guide pointed out how amazing it all was, "One floor broker could be holding an order transmitted all the way from London. The floor broker standing right next to him could be holding an order all the way from Hong Kong." Sarcastically, I loudly observed "The thing that is amazing is that you are preventing those two orders from matching until a human-being taps his keyboard." Suddenly, everybody around me stopped what they were doing and stared at me. My tour guide quickly ushered me out of the building. I got kicked out of the New York Stock Exchange!

Regional Exchanges

In addition to the NYSE, there were several 'regional' stock exchanges. Among them were Boston, Chicago, Cincinnati (ironically, also located in Chicago), Pacific Coast, Philadelphia, and the American Stock Exchange (AMEX). The oldest, Philly, was founded in 1790, two years before the NYSE.

Because of the Unlisted Trading Privileges Act, a stock listed on any stock exchange could be traded on any other stock exchange. The Consolidated Tape System (CTS) was created in 1976. It replaced the old NYSE ticker tape system. With CTS, each exchange transmitted their best bid and offer. The CTS system distributed the bids and offers from each exchange. Brokers paid to receive the consolidated quote feed. Regardless of which exchange it came from, the highest bid and the lowest offer, was referred to as the National Best Bid Offer (NBBO).

Brokers had a common-law duty of 'best execution'. This required them to try to find the best price for their client. In practice, a broker had three choices, they could either: 1) route the order to the market showing the best price, or 2) route the order to another regional exchange that agreed to match the best displayed price, or 3) route the order to an over-the-counter dealer who agreed to match the best price.

During the 1990s, it was highly valuable to trade against retail customers. Firms paid hundreds of millions of dollars to 'take the other side' of orders from customers of Ameritrade and Schwab.

The wider the spread was, the more money the dealers, specialists, and floor traders made. Almost everyone in the industry had an incentive to keep the cartel in place.

Stocks were sky-rocketing during the dot-com era, so the public usually made money trading stocks even with the wide bid-offer spreads. After the dot com bubble burst, traders began to be more concerned about market efficiency.

Nasdaq
Nasdaq began trading on February 8, 1971. NASDAQ is an acronym for the National Association of Securities Dealers Automated Quotation System. When it was first designed, the Nasdaq system only electronically distributed quotes from competing dealers. You had to telephone a dealer to place a trade. In 1984, Nasdaq created the Small Order Execution System (SOES) as an optional way for dealers to automatically fill orders of less than 1,000 shares. During the 1987 stock market crash, dealers simply quit answering the phones. In response to SEC pressure, Nasdaq made the use of SOES mandatory for all its dealers.

Mandating SOES was a big step forward. For the first time, the public could reliably get a near instantaneous fill for up to 1,000 shares. Some brokers like Datek started catering to a new breed of day traders which came to be known as 'SOES Bandits'. The old cartel was starting to crack.

I called Nasdaq to see what it would take to get connected to their system. At first, they sounded cheerful and asked questions about Tradebot and our business model. However, their tone quickly changed when they found out Tradebot traded our own money and did not have customers like the online brokers. We were once again out of luck.

Electronic Matching

It is far easier to match buyers and sellers with a computer. A computer system, commonly called a 'matching engine', maintains an electronic book of bids to buy and offers to sell. Each time a new order comes in, the matching engine compares its limit price to the limit price of the orders already on its book. If a match is found, a trade occurs. If not, the unfilled order is added to the electronic limit order book.

With a computerized matching engine, everything is fair. All customers play by the same rules. There is no advantage to being physically on the floor. You can be anywhere in the country and trade.

Matching orders by computer is far cheaper than maintaining a physical trading floor. In the late 1990s, a new breed of matching engines started popping up called Electronic Communication Networks, or ECNs. Some of the early ECNs included Island, Archipelago, and Instinet.

The SEC established the regulatory framework for ECNs in 1998 by releasing Regulation ATS. ATS stands for 'Alternative Trading System'. ECNs are a type of ATS.

The Island ECN

Island was founded in 1996 by Josh Levine and Jeff Citron. It was originally part of Datek, an online broker. Island was spun off and became a separate company in 2000. Matt Andresen became Island's CEO. Josh Levine and Will Sterling were the main software developers. Attorney Cameron (Cam) Smith helped with strategy and business development.

I vividly remember my first visit to Island. My reception could not have been more different than my initial introduction to NYSE and Nasdaq. Island was located in a non-descript building at 50 Broad, just down the street from the New York Stock Exchange. Instantly, you could tell that Island was a scrappy tech company like us. Computers and data lines were crammed into every corner of their offices.

Cam greeted me warmly as I stepped off the elevator. He was roughly my age. We stepped into his small office. I told him we were working with Interactive Brokers as a retail customer. Tradebot had just started routing orders to Island through Interactive Brokers.

"What can Island do to get more orders from you?" Cam asked. I wanted to know more about Island and how the system worked. He was happy to tell the Island story. Cam was an expert in market structure. "So, if you don't mind me asking," Cam continued cautiously, "The name 'Tradebot' has me curious. What do you guys do?"

"Well", I replied, "We build trading robots."

"Cool." Cam wanted to learn more. "Come with me, you've got to meet the gang."   He quickly took me into a small room and introduced me to Matt Andresen. Josh Levine and Will Sterling looked up from their keyboards and joined the conversation. Matt, who was never shy, got the conversation rolling, "So, what do you do?"

 "Well, Tradebot is a small firm with six people in Kansas City. We are working with Interactive Brokers as a retail customer – which enables Tradebot to route orders to Island. We are doing a couple million shares per month, but hope to do more. Tradebot is all about automation. We take in the quotes, and immediately spit out orders, without a human ever hitting the keyboard. We send thousands of orders per day."

I hit a nerve. Matt was immediately overflowing with huge excitement,

"Wow, we built Island for people like you!"

"What can we do to get more orders?" Josh jumped up and furiously started diagramming the Island system on the whiteboard. The conversation quickly got very intense. All four guys, Island's top four executives, were so curious about everything I was proposing. They all started firing off questions in rapid succession. I was explaining everything as fast as I could, talking a mile a minute. The fast-paced conversation continued for about an hour. It was like I had stumbled upon my soul-mates. These guys got technology. They got trading. They were nice. They got straight down to business. They cared about ideas more than pedigree.

As we were winding down the meeting, I reminded Matt that we had a retail account and were just doing a few million shares per month. I asked Matt why the big interest. I was not expecting so much attention.

He said, "For two reasons: One, we have theorized bots would be making markets someday, but no one using them has ever stumbled through our front door, and two: In this business – if you are smart – you will be big soon enough."

Matt continued with his fatherly advice,

"Look, in this industry, money follows ideas."

"You have amazing ideas. The money will come soon enough. I have no doubt. There are total dumb-asses managing millions up and down the street. I'd rather spend my time with someone smart."

It was just the pep talk I needed. I flew back to Kansas City excited about doing more business on Island.

Over the next several months, I had several great one-on-one phone conversations with Matt, Cam, or Josh. We debated everything from technology architectures to optimal pricing increments. Each of these three men taught me so much about the industry. I developed a deep sense of respect for Island.

Island was generally thought of as anti-establishment by the big firms on the street. They had a bit of a chip on their shoulder. Island had spun out of Datek, which was looked down upon as a shop catering to day traders.

Island's main strength was its technology built by Josh Levine and Will Sterling. Simply put, the Island system was better architected than the much more expensive systems run by Nasdaq. On occasion, Josh would challenge Tradebot to send him hundreds of orders per second to test how fast Island could process them. For him, it was a mark of pride. Island wanted to be the fastest. None of the other markets even came close.

Archipelago (aka Arca)

Archipelago (literally meaning a collection of Islands) was the other big ECN in those days. It was started by CEO Jerry Putnam as a spin-off from brokerage firm Terra Nova. In Chicago, their office was only about a block from Getco. This was the dot com era and they had received major funding from respected industry players such as Goldman Sachs. One of their early investors was also American Century in Kansas City. Mike Cormack left American Century to be the firm's president. He and I got along well from the start.

Arca's strengths were relationships and marketing. Jerry was such a nice guy. He was also a huge racing fan. Arca sponsored an Indy Car with the Andretti Green racing team. Every spring, they would invite their best clients to Indianapolis for the race. The night before the race they would throw a big party in the garage. Arca race events were a great chance to meet some of the people we were trading against.

Tradebot connected our system to Arca and began sending orders. As we made enhancements to our software, we gave updates to Getco, who had also started trading on Arca.

Nasdaq SuperMontage
People trading Nasdaq stocks looked at what was called the 'Nasdaq Level 2 display'. Each dealer had a four letter acronym. For instance, Goldman Sachs appeared as GSCO. Island was ISLD. Archipelago was ARCA.

If you wanted to trade on Island or Arca, you could either send the order directly to them, or you could send it to Nasdaq. The Nasdaq SuperMontage system had a feature called 'Order Delivery' that would forward the order to Island or Arca if they were showing the best price.

Because of Order Delivery, all we had to do was make tighter quotes on Island or Arca. Everyone watching the Level 2 quote would see ISLD or ARCA on the inside. If Nasdaq got the orders, they would forward them to the ECNs.

Stock Models
Our initial stock trading models were primitive. We tried lots of new ideas. Many of them did not work. It was hit or miss.

In late 2000, we made a major breakthrough. Standard & Poor's publishes a widely followed index called the S&P 500. Both futures and stocks are traded based on the same underlying index. The underlying stock traded on the AMEX under the ticker symbol SPY. The CME licensed the rights to the futures product. The electronically traded futures product was called the CME E-Mini S&P 500, ticker symbol ES.

In those days, it took separate accounts to trade stock and futures, and few people did both. We noticed that a move in the ES would usually cause a similar move in the SPY a fraction of a second later. While it was only a fraction of a second, the lead-lag relationship was visible to the naked eye on our charts. If our systems could react fast enough, this trade might be profitable.

SPY

Most SPY trading took place in the AMEX pit. The pit was totally useless to us. During the time it took to get your order into the pit, the floor traders would move the market against you. At AMEX, the minimum tick size between bids and offers was $1/16^{th}$ of a dollar ($0.0625). With wide bid/offer spreads, the floor traders made a fortune. Someone once told me that the biggest trader in the AMEX S&P pit made over $50 million in 2000. Great for them, not so great for the public who were being ripped off.

You could also trade SPY on Island, outside of the AMEX pit. Island was fully electronic. There was no trading floor to slow things down! At Island, you were allowed to trade in penny ($0.01) increments. (For a while, you were even allowed to trade in sub-penny increments, but this practice, with a few exceptions, was outlawed by the SEC in 2005.)

We placed bids and offers on Island in SPY based on prices in ES. When ES went up, we raised our bid. When ES dropped, we lowered our offer. We figured out a mathematical ratio between SPY and ES prices.

At first, our new SPY trade was like shooting fish in a barrel. Money started to fall from the sky. It was amazing. Our trading volume started to climb quickly.

However, the easy money did not last long. The trade quickly became much more competitive. Recall that our contract with Getco required us to share all our trading models with them. So, about one week after we

43

invented it, we shared our new SPY trading models with them. Getco connected to Island about a week after we did. They massively cranked up the size and also profited from the trade.

I always wonder how much money we would have made if we had been able to keep the SPY trade to ourselves instead of sharing it with Getco.

5. Decimals

Before electronic trading, the bid-offer spread was wide. It was profitable to be a pit trader or a specialist. You could buy at the bid and sell at the offer, making a nice profit on the spread.

It was a huge edge, but for some insiders, it was not enough. They got greedy. It was not uncommon for pit traders or the old Nasdaq market makers to pressure each other to keep the spreads even wider than the minimum increment.

There were huge scandals. In 1989, the FBI did a sting in the futures pits in Chicago. It resulted in 46 traders being indicted on 1,500 counts ranging from racketeering to fraud. Separately, in 1998, 24 Nasdaq market-makers settled a bid-rigging lawsuit for $1 billion.

Change to Decimals

Under pressure from the SEC, the industry was forced to switch from quoting stocks in fractions to decimals. Penny increments were no longer just for Island. All the stock exchanges like NYSE, Nasdaq, and AMEX were forced to change their minimum trading increment from $1/16^{th}$ of a dollar ($0.0625) to a penny ($0.01). Many in the industry failed to understand the implications of the shift from fractions to decimals.

When the SEC announced the change, I knew instantly the impact would be enormous for two reasons. First, it collapsed the spread by 84%. Smaller increments allowed automated traders like Tradebot and Getco to tighten the spread, saving investors huge amounts of money. Second, it accelerated the shift from floor-based trading to electronic trading. There was no way the Nasdaq dealers trading manually on keyboards or traders on the floor could keep up. This was amazingly good for investors, but not so good for the old pit and floor traders. I knew at that moment:

"The cartel was going to be crushed."

45

NYSE and Amex made the shift to decimals in January 2001 and Nasdaq converted three months later.

The New World Order – Spreads Collapse

Automated trading firms like Tradebot and Getco were on the rise. Other firms like Automated Trading Desk (ATD), Tower, and Citadel also developed algorithms.

We could now compete by aggressively tightening the spread. The labor cost of supplying liquidity to the market had dropped to the point where only the most technology savvy firms could compete.

The public saves billions per year with the tight spreads that came about as a result of market automation. All the major academic studies confirm that the cost to implement a trade has plummeted. Unfortunately, few people realize how much the public has benefited from electronic trading and tight spreads.

SPY was then the highest volume stock. Before long, with the intense competition between Tradebot and Getco to tighten the spread, the majority of the trading volume in SPY shifted from the inefficient, manual AMEX pit to Island's automated matching engine.

Island volume grew sharply. The growth in volume attracted more and more firms to connect to Island and trade. Island ran a full-page ad in the *Wall Street Journal* announcing they had passed Amex in terms of volume traded. Electronic markets were gaining traction quickly.

Commissions & Rebates

Even though our trading volumes were growing exponentially, our profit per share traded was falling dramatically at the same time.

At this point, we were still retail customers. We had to pay a commission on each trade we executed. When we started with Interactive Brokers, our commission rate was a penny per share ($0.01). Tom Ascher, our account manager, told us they would rebate half of the commission if we traded 5 million shares per month or more. This was great. Now we could crank up the volume even more. There was only one catch. They never told us <u>when</u> we would receive our rebate.

Sometimes it took several weeks after the end of the month before we received our rebate. As a small cash-strapped company, we needed the cash flow to continue trading. Despite Tom Ascher's pleas on our behalf, there was no way to get our rebate from IB until the owner, Thomas Peterffy, personally signed the check. To this day, I still do not understand why it took them so long to send us our money.

Blackwood

In spring 2001, after a few months of nail-biting over cash flow, we found another firm with an API. Blackwood was a day-trading shop in lower Manhattan. Our commission dropped to $0.00335 per share – in real-time with no rebates to work around. Besides SPY, we started trading tech stocks like Microsoft, Intel, and Cisco. Our average daily trading volume continued to grow.

Blackwood's computer system was designed to support a roomful of traders hand-typing orders on keyboards. Our automated trading system could easily generate far more orders per day than thousands of manual traders. Blackwood was glad to have our business, but they were choking on our volume. We often had to throttle things back to avoid crashing their systems.

9/11

No one imagined what would happen on the morning of September 11, 2001. We were doing some small pre-market trading, when we saw the market gap down. We closed our positions. Trading was halted shortly thereafter.

We flipped on the television in time to see a second plane hit the World Trade Center. Blackwood was only a few blocks from the twin towers. I called our account manager to see what was going on there. He sounded very shook up. "We are under attack!" he yelled and quickly hung up the phone. We were 1,197 miles away, but I was still stunned. Things in New York were far worse. Many innocent people lost their lives that day.

I went home early. I spent the rest of the day and evening just glued to the TV watching the replays unfold. The world would never be the same.

The market stayed closed for the rest of the week. The following Monday, America cheered as the firefighters rang the bell to reopen the markets. "God Bless America" was playing. It was a rough day, and the Dow dropped a record 684 points. Bob Pisani from CNBC said, "Just getting the markets open is a victory." The markets were extremely volatile for the rest of the month.

Broker Dealer

As our trading volumes grew, the trading commissions owed to our brokers grew as well. One month, we grossed $3 million and paid $2 million in commissions. There was no reason our brokers should be making more money on our trades than we were. We had to figure out how to become our own broker-dealer.

I asked Cam Smith at Island whether it was possible to set up our own broker-dealer. He said it wasn't really that hard if you became a member of a regional stock exchange like the Pacific Coast Exchange (PCX). Within a few weeks, we filled out the application and got approved as our own broker-dealer. We no longer had to pay commissions, but we still had to pay transaction taxes and exchange fees. As our costs dropped, we kept trading more and more. We expanded the list of symbols we traded.

Getco Split

Getco, which had started the same month as Tradebot, had expanded even faster. From the start they had access to millions in capital and they grew their headcount faster than we did. Being in Chicago helped, but more important was their global vision. From the very beginning, Dan saw all markets globally interconnected.

Dan decided to move to London to help launch Getco's international expansion. Getco had a number of different divisions doing different trades, but the biggest one was based on the software licensed from us. They were coming up with new trading ideas at breakneck speed. My small team of programmers just could not keep up.

I told them in order to expand more rapidly they needed to hire their own group of programmers and develop their own code. I proposed that we unwind the deal that had helped launch both our firms. Tradebot sold Getco a royalty-free world-wide copy of our source code in exchange for $500,000 and the shares they owned in Tradebot (about 14% of Tradebot).

Steve Schuler was skeptical at first, but I was persistent. Neither Dan nor Steve had a programming background. They even sent their first IT manager, Rob Smith, down to Kansas City as part of his interview. I told them he would be great and they should hire him on the spot – they did.

We delivered the final copy of our program and source code to Getco in January 2002. We parted ways. We were now competitors and would no longer share our trade secrets. Over the next seven years, Getco expanded globally and entered several new asset classes. Watching from a distance, the growth of their firm was amazing.

Getco helped launch Tradebot, and Tradebot helped launch Getco. They were our biggest competitor. I always looked up to Getco. They showed me what was possible in our industry.

Sole Shareholder

The dot-com crash was brutal. From its peak in March 2002, the Nasdaq market lost over 80% of its value by the end of 2002. During the same time period, Tradebot investors did pretty well.

After we bought out Getco, I owned over 90% of Tradebot. In the spring of 2002, I bought out the remaining Tradebot shareholders. People with founders stock like my dad, Tom, and Craig received over a thousand times their initial investment. Investors who bought into our private placement round in 2000 at 37 cents received more than three times their money for their two year investment. Not bad for a company unworthy of 'professional investment'.

I have been the sole shareholder of Tradebot since 2002.

Co-location

Over time, the technology of the markets kept getting faster and faster. The time it took to send an order dropped from tenths of seconds to thousandths of seconds (milliseconds).

The speed of light from Kansas City to New York is about 6.75 milliseconds. By 2002, the systems were getting fast enough that this delay was becoming a problem.

Being in Kansas City, we were at a disadvantage to firms in New York. I spoke to Cam Smith at Island about our dilemma. He said there was a telecommunications company upstairs from them. We called them and arranged to rent rack space so we could put our servers in the same building as Island at 50 Broad. I was told that they ran a fiber optic line down the back staircase.

This was one of the first instances of co-location (co-lo) in the industry. It was not long before other electronic trading firms such as Getco caught on and started using co-lo's too. It no longer mattered if you lived in Manhattan or Kansas City. The playing field was now level.

Wedbush

All stock trades in the United States are cleared and settled through the Depository Trust and Clearing Company (DTCC). This allows you to buy stock on one exchange and sell it on a competitor. Most small broker-dealers are not direct members of the DTCC. Instead they use the back office clearing services of a larger broker dealer, commonly called a clearing company.

Wedbush Morgan was a regional broker based in Los Angeles. They were focused on full-service retail and high-net worth brokerage. They also did investment banking in manufacturing and other old-line industries. They were a 50-year-old traditional firm that had avoided the whole dot com mania that swept the West Coast. Many of their once cool competitors like Robinson Stevenson had imploded in the dot com crash. Left standing, Wedbush was in the interesting position of being the largest West Coast investment bank.

They had recently hired an entrepreneurial guy named Harvey Cloyd.

Harvey had owned his own market maker on the PCX until penny increment trading caused spread compression and forced his firm out of business. Harvey thought Wedbush was well positioned to grow its clearing business by catering to high-frequency trading shops like Tradebot.

Harvey had been calling on our firm for a few months, but was unable to win our business. He offered Tradebot very aggressive flat rate based on our expected volume. Tradebot ultimately agreed to move its clearing business to Wedbush. Unfortunately, this deal did not last long.

Tradebot's volume was much larger than anything Wedbush had cleared before. When Harvey was quoting our rate – he left out some costs that seemed insignificant, but when multiplied by our huge volume, turned out to matter a great deal. In a panic, Harvey, his boss, and his boss's boss called us with the bad news – after one month they would be forced to close our account. Even though the contract did not require it, I told them we would make them whole on the costs they incurred on our behalf. We renegotiated a cost-plus arrangement that worked well for both firms. By being flexible, Tradebot built a valuable relationship with Wedbush.

I traveled to Los Angles to meet the Wedbush team. Ed Wedbush is probably one of the nicest, most honest people in the securities industry. After growing up in St. Louis and getting an engineering degree, he moved out to L.A. and hung out his shingle. Fifty years later, a twelve story building proudly displayed the Wedbush name and Ed Wedbush was still at work on the trading floor of the company that bears his name. Before meeting Ed, several of the managers warned me to be careful not to cuss in his presence. That's just the kind of straight-laced guy Ed was. Ed's two sons, Gary and Eric, were also involved in the business. Eric ran a venture capital fund and Gary headed up their capital markets division.

Over the next several years, Harvey and the rest of the Wedbush team kept looking for ways to process our business more efficiently in order to lower our costs. We appreciated their efforts and started referring other high-frequency shops, like Getco, to Wedbush. Within a few years,

Wedbush Morgan was clearing more business than any other firm on Wall Street.

Inet

Instinet was the oldest Alternative Trading System, tracing its roots to 1967. Tradebot connected to Instinet and started sending orders in 2001. Instinet was not eager to get small orders. They were more geared towards serving the large institutional investors. We did have some success on their system, but our relationship was never as good as it was with Island or Arca.

In June 2002, Instinet agreed to acquire its fast-growing rival, Island, for $508 million. The combined company was renamed Inet, but I still refer to it is Island.

Going into the merger, there were many more staff at Instinet than at Island. It was a clash of cultures. A week after the merger was complete, Matt Andresen called me to let me know he had resigned and would be leaving. He said the internal politics were just not fun anymore. Matt joined Stanford Bernstein then later moved to the hedge fund Citadel. Josh Levine left the industry. Will Smith went to UBS. Alex Goor and Chris Concannon were promoted to fill the void. Cam Smith stayed on for a while to work with Alex on strategy. He eventually left New York to move his young family to Texas and work with trading firm Quantlab. Within a few short years, the heart and soul of the old Island team had gone off in separate directions. In many ways, it was sad for me to see the energy and spirit of this rebellious startup dissipate.

More Volume

On October 9, 2002, Tradebot reached a major milestone. That day, our firm traded over 100 million shares for the first time. We had only been in business three years. We had been trading stocks less than two years. We had been a broker-dealer less than a year. We were starting to do some serious volume.

It was a time of excitement and growth. We had six associates in May 2001, and by October 2002 we had added 11 more. The company was starting to feel like a real firm. We were beginning to make good money.

It was also a time of rapid innovation. Our trading models were rapidly changing and improving. The markets were changing as well. ECNs were competing aggressively with Nasdaq and NYSE.

Smaller Competitors

In addition to Island, Archipelago, and Instinet, the industry had a number of smaller ECNs including Brut, Bloomberg, Attain, and Trac. In time, Tradebot connected to all of them. We got to know their management teams. I gave each of them some advice about how they might want to improve their product and grow their business. I viewed the competition between markets as a very good thing for our industry. I pondered the idea of starting our own ECN, but decided it would be hard to compete with Inet and Arca.

6. Staloff Green

By 2003, business at Tradebot was humming along nicely. The move to decimals had allowed our electronic trading volumes to explode. We were making more money than ever. We thought we were geniuses. It was time to expand.

Retail Order Flow
If you are not in the industry, you might be surprised to learn that most orders from retail stock trading accounts are not sent directly to a stock exchange.

Most retail orders are instead sent to 'wholesalers'. Wholesalers usually pay other brokers for their retail order flow. If, on average, retail investors (as opposed to institutions) are profitable to trade against, wholesalers will share a portion of that edge with the retail brokers. The retail brokers in turn use this money to lower the commission for retail investors. 'Payment for order flow' is a well-established industry practice. Many studies have been done on its benefits and drawbacks. It is legal, but it will probably always be controversial.

We studied the business of the wholesalers. One of the largest wholesalers was Knight Securities. Since Knight was a public company, its financials were available. Even after making payments for order flow, Knight's profit per share traded was greater than Tradebot's.

We decided to get into the business of wholesaling.

Philadelphia Stock Exchange
Philly is the oldest stock exchange in the country. Tradebot considered becoming a member of the exchange in order to use it as a platform to become a wholesaler.

I spoke to Barry Nobel, the head of sales and marketing for the exchange. He was very helpful. He explained that Philly would be glad to have us as a member. We could just become a member on our own, but Barry suggested another possible option. An exchange member was currently for sale. He introduced me by phone to Harry Green, the head trader at Bloom Staloff.

Bloom Staloff

Bloom Staloff was a regional stock exchange member, similar to Knight, but smaller. The company had started in 1990 as a partnership between its two named founders, Jim Bloom and Arnie Staloff. Before the switch to decimals, the firm was profitable and had grown. At its peak, the company had about 50 employees.

However, after decimalization the company had been losing money and laying off traders. Bloom Staloff was not the only wholesaler in Philly that was hurting. Almost all of the old dealers on the floor were having a hard time. Many were closing their doors or consolidating.

Presiding over the demise of a once-thriving business takes a toll on any executive. By the time I met him, Jim Bloom was ready to pull the plug. He just wanted out. To keep the operation going, he and Arnie had each spent a sizable portion of the money they had made over the years. Arnie was scrambling to find a way to keep the firm afloat.

Arnie Staloff

I flew into Philadelphia and met Arnie at the airport. A short man in his early sixties, Arnie was a walking history book about the battle between the regional exchanges and the New York Stock Exchange. The year before I was born, he started his career with the SEC. While I was in kindergarten, he helped debate and draft the 1975 amendments to the 1934 Securities Act. These amendments created the National Market System and started to level the playing field between the regionals and the NYSE.

Arnie took me on a long driving tour of Philadelphia. For a lover of history like me, there was nothing quite like driving by the Liberty Bell and listening to every word of Arnie's first-hand account of our industry's history. We had dinner at the Rittenhouse, an historic Philadelphia hotel located a few blocks from the exchange. Arnie knew someone there and got me a great rate on a room.

The next day, I met the rest of the team and toured the Philly trading floor. We hammered out the framework of the deal. Jim Bloom would sell his half of the business to Arnie. Then, Arnie would sell the business to Tradebot for $100,000. Harry Green was the head trader. The firm would be renamed Staloff Green. The deal closed in February 2003.

Staloff Green

Staloff Green needed a quick turnaround. Each month, their trading profit did not cover their overhead. After decimalization, their average net profit per share traded hovered around a tenth of a penny per share ($0.0010). They were only trading about one million shares per day. Net trading income was about $20,000 per month and overhead was over $100,000 per month. On a per share basis, their basic business model worked, they were just not doing enough volume. They already had the key relationships that allowed them to receive retail order flow. The thing they were missing was good technology. With better software from Tradebot, we believed the business could scale to profitability.

After the transition, Staloff Green had six traders, one accountant, and Arnie. Harry Green managed the traders and the day-to-day trading. He was responsible for keeping our risk exposure in check. The traders worked at rented booths on the trade floor of the exchange. Arnie managed the back office operation from an office in the building next to the exchange. He was responsible for the relationships with the order flow providers.

The plan was to use Tradebot automation to ramp up the volume so we could start making money again. I individually interviewed each of the eight people who would be joining our firm. People were apprehensive about change, but excited about the prospect of finding a way to make money again. I told everyone the merger may or may not work out. If it didn't, each person was promised a two month severance.

Everyone on the Philadelphia exchange staff was extremely helpful. Sandy Frucher, the chairman of the exchange told me he was glad to see some new blood coming in. We both agreed that electronic trading was the future.

Bridge

Meanwhile, back in Kansas City, Tradebot decided to add two new developers to beef up our software team. With the added capacity, we would be able to make the changes necessary to support wholesaling.

Bridge Information Systems was another company that crashed and burned in the aftermath of the dot-com downturn. Bridge was founded in St. Louis in 1974, but had a significant software development office in Kansas City. The company made ten acquisitions from 1996 to 2001, resulting in a heavy debt burden. At their peak, they had over 5,000 employees. Bridge filed for bankruptcy in February 2001. Some of their technology assets were purchased by Reuters in September 2001, but the company was clearly on the decline and downsizing rapidly.

Through a friend-of-a-friend, Tradebot was introduced to two of Bridge's key software developers, Rich Stigall and Paul Rose. Both men had grown up in Richmond, Missouri, a small town 37 miles northeast of Kansas City.

Paul was two years younger than me. In our interview, he was intrigued by Tradebot, but had a baby on the way and was not quite sure about leaving Bridge. Paul told his friend and colleague, Rich Stigall, about the interview. A bit more senior, Rich was four years older than Paul. We interviewed Rich a few days later. Almost immediately, you could sense Rich's excitement about Tradebot. He accepted a job with us and went back and told Paul. With Rich coming onboard, Paul called us back and also accepted a position with Tradebot.

Both Rich and Paul are incredible C++ developers. Their minds are highly logical, having the ability to take complex problems and break them into solvable chunks. Over the years, both men have worked on key parts of our trading systems.

Turnaround

I was on a mission to quickly turn things around at Staloff Green. Within a month of closing the deal, we relocated the six traders from the Philly exchange floor to the upstairs office. Arnie was surprised the day new computers for everyone showed up. The entire Staloff Green team now worked from the same office instead of being in separate buildings.

I flew to Philly for one week each month to help improve the acquisition. On one of the trips, Arnie and I took Amtrak to NYC. We met Pat Whalen and Tom Russo at Lehman Brothers. We also stopped at Morgan Stanley. Arnie was proud to introduce me to his friends in the industry. One of those friends was Joe Rizzello at Pershing Securities.

Arnie also introduced me to Chris Nagy at Ameritrade. Ameritrade is headquartered in Omaha, Nebraska. They were the largest provider of order flow to Staloff Green. We wanted them to send us more order flow. Arnie flew out to Kansas City and we took the three hour drive up to Omaha.

Chris and the rest of the team at Ameritrade were cooperative. They wanted to see healthy competition among wholesalers. "It's all about performance." said Chris. "If you give our customers good fills, we will continue to send you more volume. The retail customer has simple expectations. They want to pull up a web browser and see a quote. They enter an order and hit the submit button. They expect to get filled within a second at the price they saw on their screen. People try to make it more complicated, but it is not – just give them the fill they expect."

Bleeding

Despite our attempts to leverage technology, Staloff Green was still bleeding money fast – about a hundred grand a month. The problem was that it took eight people to trade about 1 million shares per day. By comparison, at Tradebot we were trading over 100 million shares per day with only slightly more people. With the slim bid-offer spreads, the labor cost per trade at Staloff Green was just killing us. We wanted to automate more, but in order to trade on Philly, you had to use their PACE order execution system. The PACE system was ahead of its time in 1975 when it was one of the first exchange systems to allow automated execution of customer orders under some circumstances. The problem was that the system was designed for floor trading and required too many manual keystrokes in cases such as locked or crossed quotes. While the Philly technology team was working on improvements, we realized they would not come fast enough to save us. Our new business model was doomed.

One Friday in May, I called Arnie with the bad news – stop trading – we are shutting down the firm. I wanted to stop trading immediately, but Arnie persuaded me to allow him two weeks to work with the firms that were sending us order flow. He said this is a very small world and you never want to burn bridges.

Tradebot put up the money to wind down Staloff Green responsibly. We paid all employees their agreed upon severance. We even had to pay the landlord to let us out of our of our lease early. Between the acquisition cost, the new hardware, operating losses, payment for order flow, and shutdown costs – *Tradebot lost just over $1 million on the Staloff Green project.*

Tradebot got in quick and got out quick. Most observers were stunned at how rapidly we made decisions. I have always considered being nimble a major strategic advantage.

We knew going in we wanted to risk about a million. This was about 10% of Tradebot's expected revenue for 2003. When we hit our stop-loss, we threw in the towel – no looking back. It was a painful lesson. It was expensive. It taught us to be humble.

Connections

Even though an expensive lesson, Staloff Green was not a total loss for Tradebot. The trading industry is a very small community and we were starting to make connections that would prove valuable down the road.

Arnie and I remained friends. He went on to set up a consulting practice with Joe Rizzello and Bill Harts (a former Nasdaq executive). He told me that on Wall Street everyone appears to be your friend when you are making money. Only the tough times reveal who your true friends are. This would not be the last time we worked with Arnie.

Enough

Near the end of 2003, I had pizza again with my mentor, Craig Salvay. I shared with him my experience with Staloff Green. We were having a pretty good year at Tradebot. Despite the setback, I had reached my goal – my net worth had surpassed the $10 million mark I had set four years before. My Tradebot stock was worth a thousand times my initial investment.

Craig looked at me and smiled. "No matter what you do from here forward – realize that you are now just playing the game for the fun of it," he said. It was the most valuable advice I have received. He left me with another question,

"Are you happy?"

The question caused me to ponder for quite a while. I realized it was time to reorganize some priorities in my life. Up to a point, making money improves your quality of life. You have the ability to provide for your family. You can live in a decent house in a decent neighborhood. You get to go on cool vacations. All of these things cost money. Beyond your personal needs, money gives you the ability to give back to the community by donating to charities of your choice. This is a good thing. More money gives you more choices.

Once you have money, why continue to work? Different people will have different answers to that question. There is no right or wrong answer. For me, I like to work and I like my team. I enjoy spending time with people who are smart and motivated. It's fun to be the underdog against Wall Street, to compete with New York, and find ways to win. My life would have been far different if I had retired in 2003. In fact, the industry would be far different.

I realized that I had 'enough' in the sense that my material needs were satisfied. Some people, often those with far more money, never reach this realization. Since 2003, I have still been making money. I make money because it is fun to make money. Trading is a game. Money is the way you keep score. In some ways, all of business becomes a big game. Money is not the ends, it is the means. I realize that. I continue to play the game not for the money, but because I love winning the game.

Ironically, once I realized I did not need the money, I started making money at a faster pace.

7. Trading Systems

Warning: I'm going on a tangent. In this chapter, I will share my favorite 35 ideas about building professional electronic trading systems. My personal narrative resumes in the next chapter.

So, how do you build a successful trading system? First, you have to define success. For me, trading success meant building a system and a company that earned a profit, day after day, for many years. For seventeen years at Tradebot, losing days have been extremely rare. Things did not happen by accident, they happened by design. My key point is:

> *"Tradebot maximized the <u>odds</u> of success,*
> *not the <u>magnitude</u> of our success."*

My goal was not to be the biggest, only the most consistent. By my definition of success, Tradebot has been successful.

Some of you may point out that there are several firms that are larger than Tradebot. You are correct. Often, I see the top earners take huge risks. One year, they pay off. The next year, they blow up. If you want to flip a gigantic coin, you might want to do that with your investor's money, rather than your own. (Some hedge fund managers know what I am talking about, right?)

1. Focus on the Core Principles
In any industry, the details change, yet the core principles stand the test of time. This chapter describes what I consider the most important fundamental concepts behind successful high-frequency trading systems.

This is intended to be a high-level overview of key concepts. The details will be different at each firm. Part of what makes the markets robust is a variety of approaches to trading.

So, for those readers considering a career in trading let me remind you this is a tough business. Success does not come easy. It takes years to build a robust trading system. The markets humble you. Mistakes cost money. Firms rise and fall. Every year, the competition gets tougher.

Tradebot does not win by being lucky. Our success is based on these key principals. Boiling seventeen years of complex systems development down into a short, readable chapter caused me to reflect on what is important and what is not. Some concepts are obvious, and some are less so.

Many people get stuck on the details of a trading strategy without first developing a good understanding of the big picture. Focus on the core principals first.

2. Law of Large Numbers

The desire to reduce risk is what led me to _High Frequency Trading_, or HFT. Rather than take big concentrated positions, we made millions of small trades per day. Most trades are only for a few hundred shares. Most positions are held less than one day.

Mathematicians call it the Law of Large Numbers. Basically, the small wins and the small losses cancel each other out. Let's say the odds of profit on a typical trade are 51%. You string together a million of these trades in a day. If the results of each trade are uncorrelated, the odds of having a winning day are something above 99.99%. Amazing!

Most people do not understand how HFT firms can be profitable day after day unless the game is rigged. The game is not rigged. It is just the mathematical characteristics of the way we have chosen to trade.

High-frequency trading is not for everyone. Done correctly, however, high-frequency trading produces far more consistent results than any other style of trading.

Throughout the rest of this chapter, when I refer to trading, I am referring to high-frequency trading.

3. The Hunt for Statistical Edge

I think of trading as a great treasure hunt. Look for situations where the odds are slightly in your favor. This is _statistical edge._ Never feel required to trade. Trade only when there is an edge. When unsure, trade very small or not at all. If a system works on a few stocks, try it on more stocks.

Look for situations that occur many times a day, and systems that can be tried on a large variety of stocks. The larger the number of trades per day, the quicker you can tell if you have statistical significance. The faster you iterate, the faster you improve.

Conversely, we do not spend too much time on events that happen only a few times per year, like the release of economic reports. Even if a good strategy could be created around these events, trading big size would be necessary to make it worthwhile. If something went wrong, our losses would be magnified. We would rather focus on small things that happen with higher frequency.

4. The Trend is Your Friend

The oldest cliché in the trading business is also the most important,

"The trend is your friend, until it ends."

If the market is going up, we want to be long. If the market is going down, we want to be short. In many cases, the odds of the trend continuing are slightly higher than the odds of the trend reversing. This is a key source of statistical edge. This sounds obvious, and you are probably thinking duh, of course. I cannot tell you how many times I have seen firms try to catch a falling knife. It's the fastest way to get bloody.

The hard part is determining when a trend starts and when it ends. There is no universal rule that works in all cases. We try several rules and use whatever works. What works changes over time based on the strategies used by the other participants.

There are two basic trading styles: *momentum* and *mean-reversion*. Following the trend is momentum, and mean-reversion is the opposite.

The more momentum followers you get in a market, the more it tends to trend. The trends tend to overshoot. When a big trend ends, there is often a violent retracement in the opposite direction. If the reversals are violent enough, some momentum players cannot get out quick enough, and lose money. Mean-reversion works in these cases.

In the quest to be first to jump on a trend, we often get head-faked into moves that have no follow-through. As long as the winners more than pay for the losers, it is just a cost of doing business. If you wait until the trend is obvious, it is too late. Most of our systems are on a hair-trigger.

Sometimes the markets are dead and just seem to wander sideways within a small range and without any real conviction. We do not want to be using a trend following system in a tight, range-bound market.

I think of the market as switching between trending mode and mean-reverting (or range-bound) mode. No system works well in all markets. A great trading system knows when to switch modes rapidly based on market conditions.

5. Let Your Profits Run
Here is another old adage that contains great wisdom,

"Cut your losses and let your winners run."

In general, we usually want to ride a winning trade as long as it is running in our favor. We have tried systems that automatically close out a position after it has gone some arbitrary amount in our favor. In general, we have found that this usually hurts our results. A good portion of our profit comes from a relatively small number of our trades when we got on the right side of what turns out to be a fairly big move. If you cap your winners, you miss out on the big positive moves.

Conversely, we generally want to get out of a losing trade as soon as we have a good opportunity to exit without giving up too much edge. The first loss is usually the best loss. It happens millions of times per day. We do not get emotional about it. It is just part of the business.

By letting winners run and cutting losses, we find that our return profile is asymmetric and lopsided in a good way. The average win is greater than the average loss. When this is true, it is even possible to be profitable when slightly less than 50% of trades make money.

6. Press the Winning Trades

Paul Dow taught me when I first started trading in the commodity pits,

"Press the winning trades."

If a system is making money, we want to see if we can trade bigger size with that system. Are there more stocks we can try it on?

At some point, we find that increasing our size starts hurting our results, and we have to back it off a notch. We find that we are constantly searching for the optimal position size.

Conversely, we never want to add to our losers.

"Hope is not a valid trading strategy."

(As in '*I hope it comes back*' or '*I hope it starts working again*'). If a system is not making money, shut it off. Never, never, never double down on losers. That is the fastest way to get fired at our firm.

7. Trade Relative Value

Trading is all about getting a slight statistical edge on each trade. Most of the winning systems I have seen focus on trading something relative to the price of something else. Corn rising caused me to buy wheat. Sometimes pairs of stocks move together. Sometimes the same asset trades in multiple places. The key is to discover the correlations that are reliable enough to trade. The most obvious correlations are also the most competitive. Less obvious correlations may provide undiscovered opportunities.

8. New Information

For intraday trading, company data like earnings are less important. Here is why: most company data is released when the market is closed. A few seconds after the market re-opens, the new company data is baked into the new asset price.

Short-term trading is based on responding to _new_ information. The most valuable market data is trade sizes and trade prices. Of secondary importance are the unfilled bids and offers placed by participants that have not yet traded. Realize that in the stock market, 90% or more of the orders are cancelled before a trade is made. Therefore, trades have a much higher information content than unfilled orders.

We call potential trading signals *triggers*. For instance, a simple trigger could be a trade at a given price level. Some triggers are more complex. Triggers have different attributes. We group and filter triggers into different buckets. We analyze the strength of each bucket of triggers to determine if it will be useful in trading.

Once we determine what triggers we want to use to trade, we program our system to react extremely quickly to incoming market data. Market data arrives in packets. The system picks apart the packets and looks for triggers. If we find a trigger we like, the system shoots an order into one or more markets. The reaction time from trigger in to order out is extremely fast. For example, if the market is going up, many people will see this and try to buy. Those who do not react quickly will miss the opportunity.

9. Adding & Removing Liquidity

There are two types of orders: *liquidity adding* and *liquidity removing*. Liquidity removing orders are designed to be filled immediately by the receiving exchange. The exchange keeps an order book of unfilled sell orders (asks) and unfilled buy orders (bids). There is a bid-ask spread between the lowest unfilled ask and the highest unfilled bid.

"The trigger for a liquidity removing order must be strong enough to overcome the cost of the bid-ask spread."

Liquidly removing orders are much easier to program. When we receive a trigger we like, we send in an order and it either matches an order on the opposite side of the book, or is cancelled if someone else beat us to the market. The upside of using liquidity removing orders is that we trade at the time of our choosing. The downside of liquidity removing orders is 'paying the spread'.

Conversely, we can use a liquidity adding order. If it is a bid, it will be at a price lower than the lowest offer the exchange is showing. The upside of adding liquidity is that we collect the spread, rather than paying the spread. The downside of a liquidity adding is that you are usually trading against someone else's trigger. If someone else's trigger is uninformed, this can be profitable. If someone else's trigger is based on new information that you do not have, you may be trading at a negative edge.

Some people think capturing the bid-ask spread sounds easy. It is not. In today's market, with tight spreads and a large number of electronic traders, it is extremely difficult to add liquidity profitably. The majority of liquidity removing orders are from other sophisticated participants who are not planning to lose money trading against you.

When trying to add liquidity, you need to have very fast technology that allows you to cancel your order if the market starts moving against you. In an attempt to avoid being 'picked off', a large percentage (90%+) of the orders in the market are canceled before they are filled.

10. Humans & Bots
The best trading systems combine the strengths of humans and bots.

Bots are best at simple math and if-then logic. Our algorithms are nothing more than piles upon piles of these simple building blocks. The thing that is amazing is that bots can do each calculation in about a nanosecond, all day long, without ever making a mistake or getting distracted. If you put good data in good algorithms, you get good results. If you put garbage in, you get garbage out. There is nothing voodoo about it. The bot does exactly what we tell it to do.

Humans are better at exercising judgement. Humans can understand a situation they have never seen before, and then do something rational. In some cases the rational thing to do is to quit trading. In other cases the rational thing is to crank up the volume when things are working.

Humans are creative. The bots do not suggest new strategies.

Our whole system can be thought of as a huge pile of code with a bunch of parameters. The human's job is to set the parameters based on the market conditions and their judgement about how we should trade each day.

11. Keystrokes

We designed our system with many parameters to allow our traders to quickly change the behavior of the system. Over time, we observed the traders and looked for patterns in the way they changed the parameters. "Why did you change that parameter?" we would ask. In many cases, we could construct a moderately complex algorithm based on what a rational trader was doing with certain parameters. We would then add this algorithm to the bot, eliminating the need for monotonous keystrokes.

Year after year, our system keeps getting more complex, and more powerful. Each time we added an expert system on top of the basic parameters, our traders got more productive.

Traders run a number of bots at the same time. For the first few years, traders launched each bot with the keyboard. Over time, we designed automated programs to launch bots with parameters based on complex calculations.

12. Gross & Net

Gross profit is the sell price minus the buy price on a trade. *Net profit* is the gross profit plus or minus all of the variable costs incurred to make the trade. Net profit includes things like exchange fees, liquidity adding rebates, exchange volume incentives, clearing fees, stock loan costs (for short sales), and government transaction taxes (Section 31 fees).

Our systems are based on net profit, not gross. It is extremely important that we bake our exact costs into our models so we can make rational decisions with all of the relevant information. When I refer to a 'winning trade', I am referring to a net winning trade. It is extremely important to get the calculations as accurate as possible It is all about the net.

13. Cut Trading Costs

We do everything possible to cut our trading costs. If you are using a broker, look around and find one with very low rates. I am amazed at how people spend hours and hours designing their trading strategy, and then pay inflated fees. Every dollar you spend in commissions reduces your net. Do not overpay. Once we got big enough, we became a broker-dealer ourselves so we no longer had to pay commissions. Once we got bigger still, we became self-clearing, reducing the cost of clearing and settling our trades.

Then we went two steps further. First, we constantly bugged the exchanges and ECNs to cut their rates and increase their rebates. We encouraged a price war among competing markets, and the entire industry got lower fees as a result. Second, we started a whole new stock exchange to escalate the price war (more about that in Part Two). We take trading costs very seriously.

14. Data Driven Decisions
We built a culture where decisions are based on robust data analysis.

It does not matter whether an idea comes from the CEO or the guy we hired last week, if the data supports the strategy, we use it.

Over the years, technology improvements have allowed us to retain more and more data at a cheaper cost per byte. We use a cluster of computers and an open source software framework called Hadoop. The amount of data we can store reaches into multiple petabytes.

Traders have ways they like to crunch the data and we have built 'cluster queries' that do this analysis. The amount of data we can crunch today is truly amazing compared to what we started with in 1999.

15. Controlled Testing
In the early days of Tradebot, traders relied more on gut feel and intuition to set system parameters. Several years back, we switched to a more structured methodology. Basically, we divide a bucket of symbols into two groups labeled 'control' and 'test'. We make changes to the test system parameters and leave the control parameters unchanged. Then, we randomly flip-flop the stocks back and forth between the control and test systems, usually for ten days. We throw out any extreme outliers, and look at the results. We want to know whether a parameter change helped or hurt our results. Though the methodology is not perfect, it is fairly advanced. We have been improving our testing methodology to be more useful and statistically robust.

16. Simplicity

When testing a system change, the test and control systems often have similar results. We have a saying,

"Tie goes to the simpler."

A simpler system is easier to maintain. Each change must improve the system by enough to justify the added complexity.

Over the years, we have added many features. Some are no longer used and are disabled based on parameter settings. Once a year or so, we go through the code and chop out features we are not using.

A certain amount of complexity is necessary to build a good system in today's market. However, too much complexity is expensive in hidden ways. I am always looking for ways to simplify things down to the core concepts.

17. Volatile & Non-Volatile Markets

The economy and the markets drift between periods of anxiety and periods of relative calm. Models that work well in high volatility environments may not work as well when the market calms down. The key is knowing which parameters to run in which markets.

If the market is sideways and lifeless, there are simply fewer trading opportunities. As a trading company, it's just less fun to trade in these market conditions. There isn't much we can do about it. We do not try to force trades in low opportunity markets. We spend the extra time on deep research and adding new features. Volatility will return, and we want to be ready.

In high volatility markets, there are greater opportunities and greater risks. In general, when things are working well, we try not to make big changes to the system. Just smile, let the systems run, and go home happy.

18. Be Here Tomorrow

A trader's first job is to always make sure we are in business tomorrow.

This is an important part of our company culture. Every single person in our firm has the authority to halt trading if they believe there is a problem with our system or the quality of the market data we are receiving.

As I stated earlier, <u>hope is not a valid trading strategy.</u> Our system relies on good input data and correct calculations. If we have any reason to question the integrity of the system, we disable either part of the system or the whole system depending on the circumstances.

During the last seventeen years, there have been a handful of times where market volatility has reached crazy levels. Our systems can handle a lot, but there are extreme cases where the normal rules can break down. In those cases, we either trade smaller size or, in rare occasions, completely shut off.

"When in doubt, pause."

No one should be forced to trade in crazy markets. It is often best to just step back and let things settle down. Huge moves are often based on the release of a major news event. Finding the new rational price level takes human judgement, not runaway bots.

19. Special Situations
A smaller case, but also important, are situations like federal reserve announcements and unemployment report releases. When you are analyzing data, it helps to throw out these outliers.

Right after a company releases earnings is also a special situation that needs to be handled differently. Options expiration and index rebalancing days can also be unusual. The first and last minute of the trading day can also have patterns that are unlike the rest of the day.

20. Hire the Best Technology Guys
A great trading system starts with a great technology team. The best developers are at least ten times more productive than average developers. The most valuable developers to Tradebot are the ones who also love trading and the markets.

Hiring great developers is not easy. Software Engineers are in high demand. It takes a strong culture to retain talent. I will have more to say about associates and company culture in part three of the book.

When I started in 1999, the industry was much simpler. I wrote the first profitable bot in three months working alone. I pulled several all-nighters. I was 29 years old and at the top of my game technically. It is still possible to start a one-man trading operation. Many good trading firms fleshed out their initial approach with a one or two key developers. However, you quickly learn the game is complicated and you need more resources to be competitive. So start alone and then find some smart friends. And get some rest - the all-nighters are not really that productive.

21. Traders & Technology
Success in high-frequency trading depends on traders and technology.

Software Engineers and traders are wired a bit differently. We do everything we can to foster communication between our departments. The wall and the door between our developers and the trade floor is literally made of glass. We put the coffee pot on the trade floor side to encourage the developers to occasionally get up and interact. These are small things, but they set a tone that our developers and our traders need to work together.

We encourage our traders to learn basic programming. We encourage our developers to learn about our trading strategies. Over the years, some associates have developed a deep knowledge of both technology and trading strategies. These associates are some of the most valuable in our organization. We are always looking for ways to cross-pollinate trading and development.

22. Check Egos at the Door
Good traders are often very competitive. Competitive people tend to have strong egos. However, the decision making must be data driven rather than ego driven. It does not matter who suggests an idea as long as it makes money. Losing money humbles a trader. The longer you trade, the more humble you become. You realize that no one knows more than the market. If your wonderful theoretical model does not agree with the market price, there is a very good chance the market is taking something into account that you are not. More than one Nobel Prize winning economist has blown up a trading firm in a spectacular

fashion.

Our culture is very different from organizations that compartmentalize knowledge and only share things on a need-to-know basis. At Tradebot, we all work on the same trading system. There is a common bonus pool. We work as a team. In general, all associates have access to all trading data. Anyone can ask questions. I ask a lot of dumb questions and occasionally a few good questions.

23. Many Theories

Over the years, we have tried thousands of small changes to the system. The vast majority of these did not work. When we fail, we fail quickly and move onto the next idea. The culture of the firm must be such that traders have the confidence to suggest new ideas.

When a trader proposes a new idea, it's often hard to tell whether it will work or not. Sometimes, you just have to code it up and try it. We try lots and lots of ideas that do not end up working.

When trying a new idea, we test it by trading small at first. If the idea does not produce, our losses are small and the time spent on it is short. On the other hand, if the idea works, we ramp up the size, the number of stocks, and the time we spend on it. A winning improvement works day-after-day. There is an asymmetric risk-reward ratio in trying new ideas. Even if only a few ideas turn out to be winners, the magnitude of the winning improvements is much greater than the cost of several traders constantly trying new ideas that don't pan out.

I think it's this ability to adapt that has kept our firm profitable over the years. The market and our models have gone through many changes. Some new traders have joined, and some people have retired, but the system keeps adapting and changing.

24. Curiosity

Every toddler is naturally curious about the world. Sadly, many adults largely quit learning after they leave school or university. Their pace of discovery slows. They seek stability.

At Tradebot, we want associates that have kept that wondrous childhood curiosity. Our environment creates a safe space to try new ideas and experiment. We want associates who are self-driven and self-taught. We want people who are constantly reading from a variety of sources. Not everyone is comfortable in this environment. There is a constant stream of new ideas.

I like to surround myself with people who are smart and thoughtful. We are always asking, "What if we tried…". Many ideas do not pan out and are put on the back burner. This is fine. A few good ideas make millions, and that is a big part of the joy of coming to work each week.

25. Change Creates Opportunity

The market keeps getting more competitive. We get a strategic edge from being nimble. When systems stop working, we turn them off. There is a constant struggle to find new systems to replace the old ones. We have been pushing out new software every week for over seventeen years.

"Change creates opportunity for those that adapt fastest."

We look at change as opportunity. Exchanges often update their rules or introduce new order types. Every few years, the SEC proposes a major rewrite to the rules that govern the industry. Often, the period immediately after a rule change takes effect has been very profitable for nimble firms. We take pride in being able to figure out the implications of structural changes faster than our competitors. We can get new code into production quickly.

26. Consider Smaller Markets

The market for US equities is the largest in the world. I believe it is also the most competitive. It would be very hard to start a firm like Tradebot from scratch in today's market.

If I was starting over, I might want to focus on a smaller market first. It would be less competitive. After I had some success, I would move to the bigger markets. The bigger the market, the more competitive it is likely to be. Pick the battles you can win. The more trading volume in a stock, the more competitive it is likely to be.

27. Modular Architecture

We use a modular architecture in our trading system.

In general, it is quickest to develop new software if one developer at a time works on each executable program. If you have too many cooks in the kitchen, it slows things down. We break up the program into modules and assign each module to a single developer, if possible. Over time, developers hand off modules to others, but at any given time, there is usually a single associate working on a single module. There are common code libraries that are used by multiple modules.

Several of the modules pass data packets to each other asynchronously using TCP or UDP protocols. Having a modular architecture makes it easier to upgrade one part of the system while minimizing side effects in other modules.

28. Robustness

Any system with thousands or millions of lines of code will occasionally have bugs. We unit test and system test before we put things in production. However, it is impossible to catch all bugs before they go into production. There is always a balance between speed-to-market and the number of test cases tried.

When systems fail, and they eventually always will, it is important that they fail in ways that cause limited damage. We often design multiple overlapping risk checks and have different software developers code different parts. Robust systems design is an art - it does not happen by accident.

29. Build In Compliance

Compliance is built into the system. The rules of the market are very complex. It's difficult, but extremely important, to follow the rules at every step. Sometimes we need to ask regulators for clarification when the rules are unclear. Every order is checked multiple ways before it goes out the door. Trading is a highly-regulated industry, especially if you are operating as a broker-dealer

30. Risk Limits

Tradebot's risk limits are set by the our Board of Directors. I believe it is important that the risk limits are ultimately approved by associates who do not work on the trade floor day-to-day. Some separation of duties is good governance. Of course, traders and trading managers request modifications to our risk limits from time-to-time, and these requests are reviewed by our board.

The system has many ways to measure and limit risk. Risk is limited at the firm, account, and symbol levels. Limits are placed on the number of orders in flight. In all, there are over 30 risk limits. Each is reviewed by the board. Each is tested by the firm in production every month. We take our risk limits very seriously.

31. Circuit Breakers

Our bots are designed with circuit breakers. The circuit breakers automatically halt trading in a strategy or symbol when a pre-determined loss limit is reached. Sometimes, losses happen quickly. There is not always time for a human to notice and react. The circuit breakers need to be coded into the system and tested on a regular basis.

32. Oops Reports

There is always risk in this business. When we experience a significant drawdown, a trader fills out what we call an 'oops report'. The report outlines what happened, what we learned, and what we will do differently in the future.

"Mistakes cost money."

We want to shine light on our mistakes instead of trying to cover them up. We do not want to pay for the same mistake multiple times.

33. Limits of Simulation

Trading 100 shares live is the best simulator in the world.

When you trade, your orders have subtle effects on the other participants and their trading strategies. For this reason, I have never placed much credence in simulated trading. To be blunt, I place a near-zero value on simulated results. It is just too easy to curve-fit and build a simulation that looks great on paper, but has very little chance of working in the real world. Start small and ramp up. Use live trades, not simulations.

34. Iterative Improvement

We did not start with a master blueprint for the entire system. The system grew and evolved little by little over the years. We got simple ideas working quickly, and then added complexity only after we debugged the initial concepts.

"Success requires constant innovation."

Iterative improvement is sometimes messy. The code is not always as elegant as we would like, but at least it works. Sometimes, we take time to completely rewrite a key subsystem. We are on our fourth major version of 'the bot'. We have completely re-written it three times, in each case using the old code as a design input, but largely rewriting the new code from scratch. Between the major rewrites, there have been thousands of minor enhancements.

35. The Secret Sauce

People ask the secret of Tradebot's success. The truth is, it's not one thing. It's doing thousands of small things well.

Being in this business for seventeen years, I'd like to think I have learned a thing or two about how to build a winning trading system and a winning trading company. The two are very intertwined.

Remember, the game is very hard. There is no magic bullet. You will be trading against some extremely talented companies. The market is unforgiving. Expect losses. Be humble and learn from your mistakes.

8. Competition

High-frequency trading is extremely competitive. Competition among firms drives innovation. Trading strategies are constantly being refined. Technology is upgraded. It is an arms race. Winning requires a combination of capital, people, trading models, and technology. The game is not easy. Lots of money is at stake. Bright people are attracted to the markets. People are aggressive. People are innovative. People are competitive.

The market does not owe you anything. Every year, new companies fight to take your place. Firms rise and firms fall.

Winning strategies constantly change. New trading models are pushed out every week. The market goes through cycles. What works one year usually does not work the next.

The rules of the game are also changing. Exchanges and ECNs introduce new order types. Every few years, the SEC revises the market structure rules.

Constant Change

Tradebot's net trading profits hovered between $10 and $20 million per year from 2002 to 2005. As our profits grew, our team grew as well. We were still scrappy, but the firm started to feel more like a business and less like a garage band. There was pressure to perform, but there was also time to have fun.

Rob Alumbaugh wrote the third major revision of 'the bot'. At first, we called Rob's version the 'Rob-Bot', which eventually got shorted to just 'Robot'. We let the traders run Rob's version and my version of the bot side by side. Over time, Rob's version started making the bulk of the profits and my version was phased out.

81

My role at the firm was switching from player to coach. I was writing much less software code. I spent more time on business strategy, hiring, and managing.

In addition to Rob and I, our core development team in those years included Kelly Burkhart, Rich Stigall, Paul Rose, Marc Ritterbush, and Chris Isaacson. Most of our top executives had a background in software engineering or computer science.

In July 2004, Joe Ratterman joined our organization. Joe had been Rich and Paul's boss at Bridge. He had more executive management experience than anyone else at Tradebot. Three years older than me, Joe was athletic and had a very high-energy level. Yet, he was soft-spoken and very thoughtful. Having been a software developer early in his career, he had spent the last decade or so in management. He knew how to manage large teams of technologists, sometimes in multiple offices. At one point, he even worked overseas. When he first joined Tradebot, we did not have a specific role for Joe. We just put him on various projects. Over time, his role would greatly expand.

Most of our trading focused on Nasdaq-listed stocks and exchange traded funds (ETFs) like SPY. Little by little, the number of stocks we traded each day grew to a few hundred, and then eventually, to thousands. As our software improved, our traders were becoming more productive and could trade more stocks per person. Data was starting to become important, but traders still exercised lots of 'from the gut' judgement about which models and parameters to run and how big to make the orders each day.

Market Structure
In 2004, trading in Nasdaq-listed stocks and ETFs was far different from trading NYSE-listed stocks. NYSE-listed stocks traded mostly on the floor of the New York Stock Exchange. The quotes put out by NYSE were manually updated by specialists and were often stale. The price discovery process was cumbersome and slow for NYSE-listed stocks which limited the market share of ECNs and other exchanges. On the NYSE, it still took several seconds to get most fills. Tradebot traded some NYSE-listed stocks on Island, but we were not very successful.

By contrast, there was a healthy competition among Nasdaq, Island, Arca, Brut, and a few smaller ECNs in the trading of Nasdaq-listed stocks and ETFs. As I described earlier, if a trader had a Nasdaq Level 2 display, not only could they see the quotes from the Nasdaq dealers like GSCO and MSCO, but they could also see the top-of-book quotes from the ECNs like ISLD, ARCA, and BRUT. Order routing technology was greatly improving. A new breed of 'Smart Routers' would automatically send customer orders to the markets where they could get the best fill.

Island, Arca, and Brut were particularly aggressive in trying to draw trading volume to their ECNs. Island started paying firms to add liquidity to their order book via limit orders. These liquidity-adding orders would attract market orders from the smart routers, increasing the amount of trading on Island. The other ECNs soon copied the liquidity-adding rebate structure. Island also started offering an incentive called 'tape revenue rebates' to attract volume in the ETFs like SPY, and other ECNs soon followed. ECNs also innovated by adding new features like the 'add liquidity only order' and the 'non-routable' order types.

Every month I spoke to the senior executives at each of the ECNs and Nasdaq. I could often convince them to cut fees or increase rebates. They were all fighting for market share. They were all looking for ways to innovate.

In the industry, the majority of trading was still done on keyboards, but algorithmic trading was clearly on the rise. The *Wall Street Journal* estimated the percentage of trading done by automated algorithms grew from 14% in 2003 to 20% in 2006. I think the actual numbers were much higher, especially in Nasdaq-listed stocks and ETFs.

In 2004, the Securities and Exchange Commission (SEC) was starting to seriously think about how to update American market structure. They wanted to harmonize the rules between NYSE and Nasdaq stocks, encourage more electronic trading, and make things better for retail investors. They started working on what became known as Regulation NMS, or 'National Market System'. Many people gave their opinions on market structure.

It quickly became apparent to me that very few people really knew much about how complex distributed computer systems actually worked. Most people who passed themselves off as 'market structure experts' had gained most of their experience in the manual trading era. Manual trading at human speed is very different from electronic trading at sub-millisecond intervals.

I realized that I knew more about market structure than almost anyone. I had a unique combination of knowledge. I was a computer engineer. I had written automated trading models. I had worked with several ECNs on order types and their business models. I knew the protocols and the data centers inside out. I had purchased cutting edge computer technology. I had read the arcane SEC market rules cover to cover. I had read the exchange rulebooks cover to cover. I had read the order entry protocols cover to cover. I knew what I was talking about. Beyond the details, I also had a grasp of the big picture. I had run a profitable trading business and designed real-time risk-management systems. Ok, to be fair, there were maybe ten people in the world that knew American stock market structure as well as I did. I started participating in the market structure debate. I got invited to speak on a few industry panels.

Recall Arnie Staloff, Joe Rizzello, and Bill Harts had a consulting business. Tradebot was their first client. In 2004, Arnie, Joe, and I met in Washington, D.C. We spoke with the SEC commissioners and senior staff about the proposed Reg. NMS rules. The folks at the SEC must have been impressed with my market knowledge because Bob Colby and Annette Nazareth, two of the top rule makers, took the time to fly out to Kansas City to see Tradebot's operation and to continue our discussion. The top people at the SEC were very concerned about creating a level playing field that would benefit retail investors. Bob asked me a question that was very thoughtful:

> "I know everyone on Wall Street will game the system and act in their self-interest. What I want to know is the cumulative effects of all the actors. Is the playing field we propose stable or unstable? Fair or unfair?"

I knew game theory. Bob knew I was one person who would give him a straight no-nonsense answer. I recommended a few small tweaks, but said that overall the proposed Reg NMS rules were a big improvement over the current framework.

The biggest effect of the proposed changes would be on NYSE-listed stocks. After the rules became effective, NYSE stocks would begin to trade much more like Nasdaq-listed stocks. The NYSE floor would lose their near-monopoly on trading in NYSE-listed stocks. The advantage of being a specialist or floor broker would shrink dramatically. Electronic trading with sub-second executions would become the norm. The playing field would become level for all. After 200 years, the guys at Broad and Wall would not be the only game in town. Under Reg NMS, the new market structure would be much better for retail investors.

Expansion

Tradebot was growing and we needed more space. Briarcliff is a 600 acre sub-division built on the bluffs overlooking the Missouri river and the downtown Kansas City skyline. In addition to about two hundred luxury houses, there were three new office buildings in the complex.

Charles Garney owned the Briarcliff Development Company. Before my wife retired to stay at home with our kids, she was a surety underwriter, and Garney was one of her accounts. Charles was in his early seventies when we met in 2003. Charles graciously invited Jamie and I over to his house for a meal. Charles and his wife Patty lived in a huge mansion. We had lunch on the back deck, and the view overlooking the city was amazing.

I liked Charles from the moment we met. He was so gracious and such a gentleman. I asked him about his business. He told me the story about how he created the Garney Company and had then sold it to his employees. He was quite proud that several of them had become millionaires by owning a piece of the business they created. He took the money he received and began working on the Briarcliff development in 1994.

Charles gave me a piece of advice. He said the best people he had ever worked with he had hired straight out of college. "Get young people who are driven, with lots of talent, and give them tons of responsibility early in their career."

One of Charles protégée's was Nathaniel Hagedorn. Charles hired Nathaniel a couple years earlier when he was still finishing school at UMKC. I'm not sure what Nathaniel's official title was, but as a practical matter, he was pretty much running Briarcliff's development activities in his mid-twenties. Charles pointed out that Nathaniel was special. He just had a vision and combined it with the drive to work harder than anyone else he had ever managed.

We spoke to Nathaniel about moving to Briarcliff. The offices were very nice, but they were currently full, except for one suite that was too small for us. He said they were starting to plan a new phase that would include office above retail, but it would be a couple of years before it would be ready.

Unable to move to Briarcliff, Tradebot found expansion space in the building next to our current location. It was an old print shop located on the ground floor. We punched a large hole and connected the two buildings. It was not luxurious, but it was functional. We roughly doubled our square footage from 6,000 to 12,000 square feet. In the print shop, we installed huge air conditioning ducts to cool the computers and monitors we used for trading. It was not long until the new space was full.

I remembered the advice from Charles. Tradebot re-focused our hiring process, adding four recruits straight out of college in 2004. The first of those four was Will Bryson. A Business Administration major from the University of Missouri at Columbia (Mizzou), Will quickly became one of our best young traders. He was from Liberty, Missouri, a suburb on the northeast side of Kansas City. Will eventually married a girl he met in high-school and bought a farm north of Liberty.

I thought deeply about the type of company culture I wanted to establish. I started working on trading robots when I was 29. With Tradebot, I have tried to create the type of business I would have wanted to work for in my twenties. Even though I have gotten older, my design criteria has not changed. Our renewed focus on college recruiting has been a key part of that design.

In the News

Most of the time, I try to avoid the press, usually preferring to 'fly below the radar'. Occasionally however, when I am proud of something, I believe it deserves to get a little bit of ink.

The first time Tradebot was in the press was with the *Kansas City Business Journal* (KCBJ). Reporter Charlie Anderson had been asking me if he could do a profile on Tradebot for a couple of years and I kept putting him off. After we expanded into our new space, I figured it was now the right time. I like working with the KCBJ because they seem to appreciate entrepreneurs. They write positive stories about companies that are expanding. Other papers are too focused on the negatives.

Charlie wrote a nice profile about Tradebot and our history. The picture above the story showed me standing on the trade floor, surrounded by 24 monitors. The title was "I, Tradebot." Charlie asked me why everyone wasn't trading like Tradebot. Aren't you worried about the big firms like Goldman Sachs? I told him, "I'm not worried about Goldman Sachs - I'm worried about five 22-year olds in a garage with a rich uncle."

Five years after the story ran, Charlie called me back for an update. He had moved to Minneapolis, Minnesota and was writing for a paper up there. "How is Tradebot doing?" I replied, "Well, I'm still not worried about Goldman Sachs. I hired the five kids and became the rich uncle."

About a year after the KCBJ article ran, I got a call from Aaron Lucchetti at the *Wall Street Journal*. The WSJ ran a front page article about Tradebot and the rise of algorithmic trading. It was the first time my company received national attention. Grandma was right, someday your picture might be on the front page of the paper.

Family Trip Two

I often talk about my business with my family. They have seen entrepreneurship in action. They understand how capitalism works.

As the kids were growing up, we often enjoyed watching business-oriented shows together. *The Apprentice* featuring Donald Trump debuted in 2004. 'You're fired', was the punchline from the show. When I did something my kids did not like, they would look at me and mock, 'Dad, you're fired.' I had to explain to them that you are not allowed to fire your family.

From time to time, my business travels took me to New York City. I took the family to visit the Big Apple. We stayed at the Trump International Hotel on the southwest corner of Central Park. We walked a mile down Broadway, passing Lehman Brothers and Morgan Stanley, to see the Nasdaq Market Site in Times Square. From there, we boarded a double-decker bus and saw the rest of the city. We took an elevator to the top of Rockefeller Center. We went by Ground Zero and the New York Stock Exchange. When I talk about New York, my kids now had a mental image of the place.

Market Competition

Competition among algorithmic trading firms reduces the bid-offer spread and makes the market more efficient.

"Competition among market centers is also very important."

It reduces the fees markets can charge to match buyers and sellers. Competition among markets causes them to innovate and introduce new order types. It causes them to upgrade their technology so they can match orders quicker.

The combination of competition between participants and competition between markets has had enormous implications. Between 1999 and 2005, bid-offer spreads collapsed by 84%. The fees, net of rebates, which exchanges and ECNs charged dropped by over 90% on a per share basis. The time it took to match a buyer and a seller dropped from 23 seconds to under a millisecond! Together, these changes save investors and traders billions of dollars per year.

The period from 1999 to 2005 saw the rise of the first generation of ECNs. Unfortunately, these first generation ECNs did not last.

Public Exchanges

CME Group was the first exchange to de-mutualize and go public. They went public on December 6, 2002 raising $166 million. The Chicago Mercantile Exchange trades futures.

Archipelago Holdings went public on August 13, 2004 raising $126.5 million. It was the first stock exchange to go public.

Publicly traded exchanges are a relatively new concept. For over 200 years, the exchanges operated as mutual companies. They were owned by their members. They were operated for the benefit of their members. They charged fees only high enough to cover expenses. They did not try to make a profit.

There are advantages and disadvantages to having for-profit exchanges. On the positive side, a for-profit business has an incentive to grow. Technology is used if it cuts costs and improves customer service. On the negative side, a for-profit business has an incentive to maximize the prices it charges. The only thing that keeps this in check is true competition. The futures markets are effectively monopolies. They have no real competition and fees are higher than they need to be. The other major problem with for-profit exchanges is regulation. The securities industry is based around a model of self-regulation. The exchanges regulate the members. This worked fine when they were not-for-profit cooperatives.

"For-profit businesses with regulatory powers is a very bad idea."

Because of the Unlisted Trading Privileges act of 1994, stock exchanges are not monopolies. However, if there are too few competitors, there is a real risk they will behave as an oligopoly and not compete on price.

From 1999 to 2005, the price wars between exchanges and ECNs were intense, cutting fees, net of rebates, by over 90%. Competition worked.

Nasdaq Acquires Brut

On September 7, 2004, Nasdaq acquired Brut from SunGuard for $190 million. Prior to joining Nasdaq in May 2003, Nasdaq CEO Bob Greifeld was a senior vice-president for SunGuard. Nasdaq realized that the ECNs were rapidly eating their lunch. From Brut, Bill O'Brien, Brian Hyndman, and Brian Harkins joined the Nasdaq team.

There was a real attitude shift at Nasdaq. They started aggressively making changes. For the first time, Nasdaq was starting to act and talk like an ECN. They were trying to upgrade their technology. They started reaching out to high-frequency trading firms like Tradebot.

Reg. NMS Passed

On April 6, 2005 the SEC approved Reg NMS. Different sections of the rules were phased in between July 1, 2005 and July 9, 2007.

The passage of Reg NMS was a major change. It was the biggest change to market structure since Congress passed the Securities Acts Amendments of 1975. The industry had been debating the details of the proposed rules for over a year, but the final passage cemented the regulations.

Duopoly

Everyone knew Reg NMS would spawn major changes. What few anticipated were the two mergers it touched off.

On April 20, 2005 NYSE agreed to a reverse-merger with Arca. The 212 year old Big Board would be acquired and go public. The merger closed in 2006.

On April 22, 2005, just two days later, Nasdaq announced they would acquire Inet. The merger also closed in 2006. The Inet acquisition gave Nasdaq a competitive technology platform.

It felt like a punch in the gut when these two mergers were announced the same week. The industry was not happy to hear the news. Sandy Frucher, the chairman of the Philadelphia Stock Exchange, called it a **'duopoly'** (meaning 'monopoly of two'). I started receiving several phone calls. Everyone in the industry was concerned that these mergers would reduce competition. Competition was what had lowered our trading costs by over 90%. Were prices going back up?

The fix was in. The SEC and the Justice Department never should have approved the mergers. Clearly, the intent was to reduce competition. There was never a legitimate debate. Big firms like Goldman Sachs were advising the parties on the merger and stood to make a great deal. They really did not care about market structure. They cared about making money. Maybe I should have been worried about Goldman Sachs after all!

Once upon a time, we had Island, Instinet, Arca, and Brut. Now, they were all gone. Nasdaq and NYSE again would dominate.

There were still a few smaller competitors and the regional exchanges, but none of them were meaningful. None of them had great technology. None of them were aggressive. None of them would ever scale.

For the next month or so, I took a series of long walks. I considered the implications of the changes in the market. If something was not done, the situation did not look good. Trading fees would almost surely be going up. I thought to myself,

"Something had to be done to stop the duopoly..."

Part Two

BATS

9. Launching BATS

From the beginning, BATS was designed from the customer's perspective. This perspective is deeply ingrained in the BATS DNA. Over time, I believe this is what made BATS different from our competitors. We built the playing field we wanted to use.

We were on a mission. We wanted to restore competition between markets. Competition from Island and Archipelago caused Nasdaq and NYSE to innovate. Competition had dramatically cut the fees exchanges charged. Without aggressive competition, the trading world would become a different place, a far worse place, in my opinion.

We borrowed heavily from the Island and Archipelago playbooks. I had great respect for what these early electronic markets had accomplished. These small companies rolled out the red carpet to a small new entity called Tradebot at a time when the large exchanges looked down their noses at us. I did not want to see that progress vaporize into a couple of large corporate bureaucracies. It was time to upset the system. Game on.

I knew we were racing against the clock. Nasdaq and NYSE would need to play nice while their proposed acquisitions were pending regulatory approval. Once the approvals came, the light would turn green and they would be free to jack up prices. We had to put a credible competitor in the race in order to thwart their plans.

What's in a Name?
The name of a company is important. It becomes a handle by which the new firm becomes known. It makes a first impression. It sets a tone.

We made a list of possible names for our new organization. I chose the name BATS. It is an acronym for Better Alternative Trading System. Since I started my trading career with baseball cards, I liked the nostalgia of a baseball reference. It denoted strength. If I was going to hit Nasdaq over the head with something, why not a baseball bat?

"Crazy Dave's Discount Trading Emporium" was one of the names on the list that we did not pick. I doubt if we would have been as successful under that moniker. It does have a nice ring to it, though.

Laying the Plans

A good business starts with a good plan. As an entrepreneur, there is nothing more exciting than a blank sheet of paper. It is much easier to change things early before you get too far along. With both Tradebot and BATS, I took the time to imagine what type of business I wanted to create. I took several long walks, pondering different strategies and approaches.

In some circles, writing a business plan is considered old fashioned. For me, it was quite valuable. The first business plan for BATS was 15 pages. I updated the plan twice in the next two years. As I look back, we pretty much accomplished what we set out to do. Things morphed over time, but the key concepts were established early.

My plans included three scenarios: a downside case, a base case, and an optimistic case. I think it is important to visualize the range of possible outcomes for a business and realize what inputs have the greatest impact on the curve. Each day, drive the business towards the optimistic scenario, but consider the financial implications of the downside scenario. If you compress time, you lower the number of months you need to incur a burn rate before you reach profitability.

For a startup, the range of possible outcomes is much wider than most serious people would care to admit. In BATS' plan, the optimistic case called for 100 times the volume of the downside case by the end of year two.

At Tradebot, I had slipped into the sloppy habit of oral storytelling around my whiteboard of chicken scratches. Joe Ratterman emphasized the importance of well written plans and power-point presentations if we wanted the business to scale. I think Joe's early emphasis on professionalism in our written plans greatly improved our odds of success.

Picking Teams

Looking back, launching BATS was a "bet the company" decision. It was more risk than a prudent person would take. I was not a prudent person, I was an entrepreneur on a mission.

In order to focus, we decided to split the company into two roughly equal teams. My team would launch BATS, and Rob Alumbaugh's team would stay focused on proprietary trading at Tradebot.

We had thirty associates in June 2005. I made two lists, carefully including a mix of traders, software engineers, accountants, and managers on each team. I shared my lists with Rob. He talked me into swapping a couple names.

We then called an all-company meeting. It was time for a fork in the road. Our tight-knit group would split. The two teams would head in very different directions. There was no turning back.

As we called off names, associates moved to the corresponding corner on the trading floor. Associates were not really given a choice. They were assigned. I figured there would be hard feelings if we got into an all company debate about who was on each team. Only one person, Ken Conklin, asked if he could switch teams. Kenny was traded to BATS for 'a player to be named later'.

On my desk today sits a picture frame. The left side contains a photo of the 18 associates (including three new hires) staying at Tradebot. The right side shows the 13 associates who would launch BATS. At the Christmas party, we handed out the picture frames as gifts. Looking at the two small teams always brings a smile to my face. Both went down separate paths. Both won.

Team Tradebot

At the time of the split, Rob Alumbaugh was promoted to CEO of Tradebot. Rob had personally designed and coded the second generation "Trading Robot" that we were now using. Rich Stigall was a senior software developer and was put in charge of the engineering efforts. Eric Boles was initially assigned a role as a trader, but was soon promoted to run the entire trade floor. Rob, Rich, and Eric drove most of the design

97

improvements over the next couple years. They would often find themselves around a whiteboard discussing new potential features. If they agreed, the upgrades would be quickly coded and put into production.

The team left behind at Tradebot seemed to have something to prove. They hunkered down and made several key breakthroughs. Over the next two years, the group would grow to 20. Innovation is often greatest when you get outside of your comfort zone.

I intentionally removed myself from all day-to-day operations at Tradebot. However, I remained Tradebot's sole owner and the Chairman of the Board. About once a quarter, I would meet with Rob to discuss how things were going. I trusted him to run Tradebot as he saw fit.

Rob is a natural leader. He is incredibly smart, but also humble and incredibly fun to hang around. Everyone looked up to Rob, and there was no doubt as to who was in charge. He did an absolutely great job running Tradebot while I was gone. Trading profits grew considerably. Morale was high.

Team BATS

BATS was a spin-off from Tradebot. Recruiting the first 10 or 20 people is the hardest part of launching a new business. The first hires set a tone and a momentum. They collectively define the DNA of the new organization. Once the initial DNA is established, it evolves slowly as the firm grows, but the starting team makes all the difference in the world.

With the benefit of hindsight, I would say that seven out of the initial 13 BATS associates were amazingly talented and went on to have truly extraordinary careers. The other six were solid followers. How lucky I was to start with such a great group.

I was CEO and Joe Ratterman was COO. Our personalities meshed well. I was obsessive-compulsive and shifted focus from topic to topic. Joe was humble and consistent. I often laid out goals for BATS, and Joe made sure our company delivered.

Kelly Burkhart led our engineering efforts. He focused on the overall design, the database, and several of the back office systems. Paul Rose was our senior engineer and wrote the key part of the system – the matching engine. I have been lucky enough to manage some great engineers in my career. Kelly and Paul are two of the best. When they design something, it just works.

In addition to Kelly and Paul, Chris Isaacson and Ken Conklin were on the initial development team. They were both early in their careers; full of energy, and on a mission. Over the next couple years, it was great to see their careers bloom.

Tami Tucker led our compliance team. Five years earlier, she joined Tradebot as my executive assistant at the age of 20. She had grown so much in those five years and was now ready for a bigger challenge. As BATS grew, Tami made the most of every opportunity.

Announcing BATS

The pen is mightier than the sword. I decided to write an open email to the industry to announce the formation of BATS. I had 65 contacts on my distribution list. Over the next couple years, I sent more emails. Some were a bit edgy. Some were funny. They got forwarded all over the street. People asked to be added to my list. I discovered how to get Wall Street's attention, for free.

The next page contains my first email to the industry.

Make the Trade

From: David Cummings

Sent: Friday, June 17, 2005 1:36 PM

To: [65 names]

Subject: Launching a New ECN - BATS Trading

Dear Friends and Colleagues,

After much consideration, I have decided to launch a new ECN.

BATS Trading, Inc. is the name of the new company. BATS is an acronym for a Better Alternative Trading System.

Pending regulatory approval, we hope to be ready to go live in early 2006. We recognize that this is very aggressive, but we feel confident that significant progress can be achieved in a short time frame.

Tradebot Systems will be the technology provider.

I will initially serve as the CEO. Joe Ratterman will join me as the Vice President & Chief Operating Officer.

The matching engine will be located in a data center run by a yet-to-be-named telecommunications provider on the East Coast.

The trade desk and operations support will be located separate from Tradebot's current operation.

We have not yet determined which firm will provide clearing services.

I will provide the initial seed capital. After proof of concept has been established, the company plans to seek additional capital from a diverse group of investors. At that time, we will hire an experienced management team from the industry and open an operation center in the NYC area.

Basic limit order matching and outbounding are just the beginning. Over time, we will bring out new order types that go beyond what is currently offered. In my mind, it is all about using advanced technology to provide a win-win matching environment. We intend to establish critical mass very quickly.

I would welcome all of your input and support. Please stay tuned to www.batstrading.com for more details.

Sincerely,

Dave Cummings
Owner & CEO
Tradebot Systems, Inc.

Industry Reaction

The Street's reaction was mixed. Wall Street seems like a big place. The truth is, there are about a hundred firms that do the majority of the trading. Within each firm, there are a handful of key people who make the decisions about which stock markets they want to use. Especially in New York, these people know each other well. Many have worked together at previous jobs. Ideas spread extremely quickly. Sometimes I would blast out an email and get a reply from someone not on the list in less than a minute.

Some people believed I should go to work for an existing stock exchange rather than try to launch a new ECN. There are differences in the way stock exchanges and ECNs are regulated, but in general they do the same thing – match electronic bids and offers. Electronic markets often start as ECNs and become a stock market when they reach critical mass. In 2005, there were several regional stock exchanges: Boston, Chicago, National, Philadelphia, CBOE, and AMEX. Some, like Philly, were over 200 years old. Each was basically proposing to do the same thing – grow and restore competition among stock markets. The problem was that none had the right management and technical teams to move quickly.

More than a few people told me I should relocate to New York, and that starting a new market from Kansas City would be uphill, to say the least. My wife made it very clear that we would not be moving.

Others in the industry were encouraging. I had met John Procopion when he had worked at Island. He had recently switched to Citigroup to launch a new ECN called LavaFlow. John was great. He went out of his way to share his rolodex and introduce me around the street.

I dropped by One Liberty Plaza in New York City to visit Chris Concannon. I also got to know Chris from his days at Island. After the merger, he was now working at Nasdaq. Chris was friendly. I shared our plans for BATS with him. I could see the gears in his head turning. He took our upstart ambitions seriously. After a short discussion, he invited his boss, Nasdaq CEO Bob Greifeld, to join the meeting. Bob asked a few probing questions. I could tell Bob was not too excited by our insurrection. As we wrapped up the meeting, he said to me, "Good luck with that." I remember the tone in his voice like it was yesterday. It felt cold. I knew he would not be rooting for my success.

I went to see Matt Andresen, Island's former CEO, who was now running the equity division at a hedge fund called Citadel in Chicago. Talking to Matt was like looking in a mirror with the roles reversed. Every strategy, every price break, every feature that I had requested from Island, he threw back in my face. To him, it was like a big game. He said we both knew where all the cards were, so we might as well play them face up. I asked Matt if Citadel would connect to BATS. In his typical smart-assed way, he made some reference to Star Wars and said if every customer was like Tradebot, creating a market would be easy. Unfortunately, the big Wall Street banks do not move that fast. At best – at best – you should expect them to start thinking about getting connected in six months. So, according to Matt, I should mark on my calendar to call him back in six months minus six hours and Citadel would then connect.

While in Chicago, I also met with Jerry Putnam, the former head of Archipelago. After a transition period, he would be leaving NYSE/Arca. He genuinely wished me well, which meant a lot to me coming from one of my heroes. He offered to help in any way he could.

Paul Adcock, who was running Arca's trade desk and tech team, made it a priority to get Arca's outbound router connected to access BATS liquidity. BATS chose the Savvis data center in Weehawken, New Jersey. It was the same building that Arca was using for their matching engine, making it easier for customers to connect to us without running new telecommunication lines.

Mike Cormack and Jenny Drake are a married couple that were both executives at Arca. I walked down the hall to their offices and learned they would both be leaving the industry and 'retiring' to Vancouver. They were probably both in their thirties. It makes me sad when good people leave our industry. Mike wished me well, but warned that starting a new market would result in several arrows in your back. Jenny was more upbeat, and concluded our meeting by saying,

"We now pass the baton to you."

Race to Launch

We had only seven months from announcement to go live. There was much to be done and little time. We started having weekly Monday morning meetings. Each week, we would go around the table and each group would report on their progress. As each group spoke, you could feel a growing sense of momentum. No group wanted to delay the launch and let everyone else down.

The software team probably had the most work on its plate. They designed and built a world-class matching engine from the ground up. Beyond that, they built the quote handling systems, the clearing systems, the user interfaces, and the transactional database. They built only the required features in the initial release and added advanced features as they found more time. Unit testing and system testing ensured the system could scale.

Joe headed up much of the back office. We had to get approved as a FINRA member, fill out Form ATS, and get regulatory approval to operate an ECN. We also had to set up billing, accounting, and customer tracking systems.

Besides my emails, we did not do much marketing or sales before we went live.

Seed Money

My plan called for raising capital in stages as we hit our milestones. I provided the seed money for BATS by investing $2 million for 2 million shares at $1 per share in June 2005.

In October 2005, I went up to Chicago to meet with my old friends, Dan Tierney and Steve Schuler at Getco. By this time, Getco was one of the largest volume trading firms in the industry. I asked them if they would also invest $2 million in the startup. Steve said, "Well Dan, the first time we invested in Cummings, it turned out pretty well." Dan retorted, "$4 million or nothing." BATS accepted the $4 million investment from Getco. The round was priced at $3 per share.

I also traveled to Los Angeles to visit Ed Wedbush. BATS received a $1.8 million investment from Wedbush. Wedbush cleared the trades for

Tradebot and Getco. They also agreed to clear the trades for BATS.

Completing the round, Rob Alumbaugh, Kelly Burkhart, and Joe Ratterman each purchased a stake with their own money. We started an employee stock option program so all early employees would share in the company's success.

That was all we had, roughly $7.8 million, to launch a new market. It was enough money to last about a year. I think we burned through less than $2 million for the hardware and software necessary to get up and trading live in January 2006. Compared to the $1.16 billion Nasdaq had paid for Inet and Brut, it was a real bargain. I laughed and laughed. I was way too cocky.

Go Live

BATS went live on January 30, 2006. By coincidence, the day was also my dad's 64th birthday. The first trade was between Getco and Tradebot. The whole company stood in the developers' offices and cheered. It was an aggressive plan, but we had all pulled together and met our goal on schedule and on budget. There is a big difference between getting the ball across the goal line and leaving it on the one yard line.

By the way, on the day of our launch, Nasdaq stock closed at $46.70. It did not reach new highs until after I was no longer CEO at BATS. I have always wondered if that was a coincidence?

First Month

Nasdaq was running a matching engine called SuperMontage, or SuMo as most people called it. The matching engine displayed quotes from all the Nasdaq dealers with their four letter monikers next to their quotes. The SuMo system also allowed ECNs to quote in the system.

SuperMontage had a key feature called "Order Delivery". This meant that a liquidity provider like Tradebot or Getco could simultaneously post an order in the BATS matching engine and a copy of the order was also reflected in the Nasdaq system.

This order delivery feature was important. It made it far easier for the early ECNs like Island (ISLD) and Archipelago (ARCA) to get up and running. BATS connected to Nasdaq and "BATS" showed up inside SuMo. If someone trading at Nasdaq hit the BATS quote, the SuMo system would deliver the order to BATS.

BATS volume grew quickly at first, reaching up to 29 million shares matched in a single day before the end of our first month.

Nasdaq definitely took notice.

Briarcliff Village

First impressions are important. The moment a client or potential employee sets foot in a business, they begin forming a mental image.

BATS needed a better image, so we found new office space. I immediately thought of Briarcliff and called Nathaniel Hagedorn to see if they had space available. He told me they were building a new retail section that would have offices on top of the stores.

In spring of 2006, we moved into our new office a couple of months after we went live. Our office was on the second floor, but it walked out to the parking lot in the back. It was right next to an elegant Argentinian restaurant called Piropos. Below us was a custom men's clothier. Tivol, a very nice jewelry store, was prominent from the entrance to the park.

Our offices had a modern look. Some walls were glass, others were bright lime green. The desks and doors were birch. Our main conference room had a great view of the downtown Kansas City skyline. Management and accounting offices lined two walls. There were cubicles in the middle. Seven private offices for software developers formed a pod with a table in the middle and whiteboards all around. There was a small data center with room for about four racks of equipment. The entrance contained a nice desk for our receptionist, a television, a new BATS logo sign, and an electronic ticker tape. There was space for about 40 associates.

The new space was nice. It gave off the right image and we had some room to grow. BATS looked like a real business.

Drumming Up Business

Before BATS, I had never run a sales organization.

Shortly after BATS went live, Ken Conklin dropped by my office. He asked if I would want some help with the sales effort. I was reluctant to lose a good software developer, but we badly needed to ramp up the sales. Kenny and I dug in.

We made a list of key prospects. We split up the list by city and started visiting potential clients. The majority were in New York, some were in Chicago, and a few like Tradebot were sprinkled throughout the country.

Kenny and I made several trips to New York together. We would often work long hours. One day, my first meeting was at 6 am for coffee and my last meeting was in a bar at 10 pm. Each trip to New York lasted three or four days. We tried to visit New York every other week.

Over the next two years we put together a real sales organization with strong hires like Jon Schneider and John Denza. Kenny moved over to run business development. The business evolved, but I will never forget the times Kenny and I were just winging it around New York City.

Marketing on the Cheap

I continued sending my emails to the industry about once a month. In time, my email list grew to over 2,000 names. I'm sure the emails got forwarded to an even wider audience. It was free. I let anyone who asked join the list, including my major competitors and the regulators.

The feedback I received from the emails kept me going. I soon realized that I had hit a nerve – people were very concerned about the concentration of power between NYSE and Nasdaq and wanted an alternative. Nothing was funnier than seeing a kid from Kansas City keep poking the establishment in the eye with mouthy emails. The truth is, a lot of things I wrote in the emails were things people said privately but were afraid to put in writing.

The other thing we did was send out full size wooden baseball bats with our logo branded on them. I cannot tell you how many offices of trading managers had our baseball bat leaning in the corner. People would drop by and swing them like golf clubs and threaten to hit traders who lost money. One customer told me it drove Nasdaq nuts when they went on sales calls and saw our baseball bats everywhere. All in all, I think we spent less than $10,000 on marketing.

Nasdaq Becomes Evil

Any upstart should expect the competition to fight back. In March 2006, Nasdaq fired a shot across our bow.

I was in New York the day Nasdaq announced that they would be removing the order delivery feature from SuperMontage. This was a major shift to the established market structure. It was directly intended to hurt new competitors like BATS.

Without SuperMontage, two firms could not trade with each other unless they were both connected to the same market. Since few firms were directly connected to BATS yet, this was potentially a major setback.

We talked to some of the other ECNs that would also be affected including DirectEdge, LavaFlow, and Bloomberg. They made some calls to the regulators. Fortunately, Nasdaq had to wait a few months before yanking the order delivery feature.

The best way to unify a force is to have a common enemy. That day, Nasdaq became my sole enemy. From that point forward, I aimed all my attacks at them. My emails became increasingly antagonistic towards Nasdaq, and their leader, Bob Greifeld.

By contrast, we always had a great relationship with NYSE/Arca. They were competitors, but friendly competitors. There is no reason to fight a two-front war. My mission was to crush Nasdaq.

Two Electrical Engineers

John Thain was the new head of the NYSE, having taken over for Dick Grasso in January 2004. Before NYSE, Mr. Thain was the President of Goldman Sachs. He was a serious, high level executive. Like me, he had started his career as an engineer.

"What are two electrical engineers from Missouri and Illinois doing sitting in Dick Grasso's old office?" This was the greeting I received from John Thain at the NYSE. It created an instant rapport. Though much more senior, he treated me like a peer. We chuckled. We spoke engineer-to-engineer. We had a common enemy in Nasdaq. We had a good hour-long chat. We joked,

"The enemy of my enemy is my new best friend."

That night at my hotel, I reflected on my meeting with John Thain. Two electrical engineers running two markets. It dawned on me how much the markets had changed since 1999. The transition to electronic trading was well underway.

Earned Media
The press loves an underdog.

Randy Williams applied for a job at BATS. He looked a bit different and talked a bit different than our other associates. He was a big guy with the build of a football player. He was just a couple years older than me, but his hair was whitish-grey and slicked back. He was from New York and talked like a New Yorker, but had found himself working for an advertising agency in Kansas City.

We normally did hiring by consensus. Randy was the exception. Joe Ratterman was not too sure about Randy. I just had a gut feeling, so I hired Randy despite Joe's initial reservations.

Randy became our head of media relations. Early in his career, he had worked as an editor for Dow Jones. He knew how the big media organizations thought and acted. He had contacts. He explained that getting coverage is all about crafting a good story line.

He arranged a series of interviews for me with *Business Week*, *Forbes*, and the *Wall Street Journal*. The basic storyline was an upstart from Kansas City takes on Wall Street. In every case, the coverage was great. My favorite piece was a story in *Forbes* by Liz Moyer titled "Swinging at Nasdaq". Below the caption was a big picture of me holding a baseball bat with the BATS logo. The press loved us. It was priceless.

Randy was the only person who reviewed my emails to the industry before I sent them out. Each time, I made a hard copy draft and Randy marked it up with a red pen. Sometimes, I would type something a bit too edgy or a joke that was not really funny. He had a good feel for how things would be interpreted. I did not always take his suggestions, but I always placed a high value on his feedback.

Randy proved to be a great hire. Ten years later, he is still with BATS as their head of media relations. He and his wife moved back to New York.

National Stock Exchange

There was another significant problem with Nasdaq's pending removal of order delivery. The SEC rules for ECNs said the ECN quote had to be part of the 'National Market System', or in other words, be accessible from an exchange or the NASD ADF (ADF stands for Alternative Display Facility). The ADF existed only as a theoretical alternative. It was intentionally priced to not be cost competitive. An ECN used to be able to put its quote inside Nasdaq SuperMontage with order delivery, but that option was disappearing.

I called Joe Rizzello. I had been introduced to Rizzello by Arnie Staloff two years earlier. At the time, Rizzello worked at Pershing Securities. He had recently left Pershing and took a job as the new CEO of the National Stock Exchange (NSX) in Chicago.

I explained our dilemma to Rizzello. Somehow, I convinced him to add the order delivery feature to the NSX system. BATS had to re-write our order handling system to work with the NSX system. It was a ton of work on both our end and their end. NSX saved our bacon. Without NSX order delivery, BATS would have been up a real creek.

Summer 2006

Nasdaq dealt us a harsh blow by getting rid of SuperMontage order delivery in the summer of 2006.

We were just starting to get traction. There was a buzz about BATS in the industry. We were beginning to be viewed as a serious competitor. I was invited to speak on industry panels at conferences.

Many firms were working to get connected to BATS. The trouble was, as Matt Andresen had pointed out, it often took several months to get a firm connected once you got their attention. Technical teams had many projects to complete and it just took time to get to the top of their priority list.

With SuperMontage order delivery gone, our volume dropped. NSX was a workable alternative for order display, but unfortunately, it provided very little order delivery flow compared to Nasdaq SuperMontage.

We now faced a difficult chicken-and-the-egg problem. Firms did not want to connect unless we were big, and we could not get big unless lots of firms connected.

Our funds were also getting low. Though I never said it out loud, in my mind I began to question whether BATS would survive. We were in a real bind.

10. Go Big or Go Home

For a founder raising capital, I have seen two approaches work:

1. Start Small and Own it All
2. Go Big or Go Home

There is no middle ground. Do not try to sell 10% of your company and then run it like a family business. It is not fair to you or your investors.

If you raise serious outside money, your investors will eventually demand a 'path to liquidity'. With private equity, the timeframe is often three to seven years. With strategic investors, the timeframe can be a bit longer. As a company grows, investors usually want to bring in 'professional management'. Honestly, few founders have the skills to run a huge organization. In order to go public, underwriters like to see a market capitalization above $1 billion. Anything less and you are usually looking for a buyout from another firm. In most cases, the acquired company gets dissolved into the acquirer. Bottom line, do not take outside investment unless you expect to create huge shareholder value in a relatively short amount of time. Most businesses are realistically not good candidates for institutional investment.

There is nothing wrong with a family business (or a closely-held business). In fact, most businesses in America are small businesses. If your goal is to keep control, avoid taking outside money, especially from institutions. Bootstrap in a way that does not require much capital. At Tradebot, we had a few small investors the first three years. A significant part of our early earnings went to buying them out. I have owned 100% of the company since 2002.

Few founders start more than one successful business. I have been fortunate to have started three businesses that reached $100+ million in value. I have gone down both paths. Both work. Both have their pros and cons. Trust me, do not try to go down the middle.

If you take outside capital, you should be willing to give up control.

BATS Destiny

BATS is a business that was always destined to go public. Recall my very first email contained the paragraph:

> "I will provide the initial seed capital. After proof of concept has been established, the company plans to seek additional capital from a diverse group of investors. At that time, we will hire an experienced management team from the industry and open an operation center in the NYC area."

This is exactly how it played out. My job was to drop a snowball down a hill. As it rolled, it got bigger and bigger. In order for BATS to reach its potential, I needed to get out of the way.

Going Big

Some people avoid talking about difficult issues. I try to make 'the elephant in the room' the focus of the discussion. My style is more confrontational than some prefer. A founder's goal is not to be the most beloved. Rather, it is to force difficult decisions that move a company forward.

We went up to Getco's offices in Chicago for our July 2006 board meeting. I told the investors we were running out of working capital, it was taking longer than expected to get firms connected, and we were facing the pending removal of order delivery. Getco and Wedbush had no interest in putting up more money. In fact, they were becoming concerned about the value of their existing investment. I told them Wall Street did not have much use for a small matching engine.

"Then what do we do?" exasperated Steve Schuler. I felt like he was disappointed with me. Like I had not pushed hard enough. I forcefully replied,

"Go Big or Go Home"

Going Big meant somehow convincing the major Wall Street banks to support us. Wall Street money always comes with strings attached. I did not like the idea of getting diluted and giving up control, but it was the only way to move forward. Getco told me to approach the big banks.

Raising Capital

I considered hiring an investment banker to help us raise capital, but quickly realized we were running out of time. We probably had sixty days of working capital left. I decided to raise the capital myself.

I revised the business plan. Joe and I put together a Power Point deck. Arnie Kaplan was an attorney that helped us put together the offering memorandum. Arnie had been around the block. Early in his career he had worked for Richard Nixon's firm in New York. He was now living in Denver. I valued Arnie's wisdom and counsel. Years later, we are still friends. Somehow, I always found the right mentor at the right time.

A trip to New York to pitch potential investors was scheduled. I stayed at The Michelangelo Hotel at 51st and Seventh, midway between Times Square and Central Park.

Lehman Round

One block south of the Michelangelo was Lehman Brothers. Their headquarters at 745 7th Avenue was an impressive place. Above the entrance, three layers of large displays rotated between their logo and their marketing slogans. It was a Thursday. Lehman assembled their investment team. Alone, I entered the building for what would be the most important meeting of my life.

A couple decades ago, Lehman was a small bank. It was spun off from American Express in 1994 and had quickly grown to be the number four investment bank. There was an attitude at Lehman, especially in their equities division, of working hard to catch up with the bigger firms. They did not seem to have the big egos that I saw at some of their competitors.

Jerri Donini ran equities at Lehman. He was about my age and originally from St. Louis. We quickly built a working rapport. Mike Bleich reported to Jerry and worked on electronic trading strategies and strategic investments. Above Jerry in the organization was Bart McDade. I guessed that Bart was probably the most senior person that would need to sign off on any potential investment in BATS.

My presentation went well. They asked several hard but fair questions. I was hoping to get $6 per share. They pounded me down to $4.

Then the conversation took a turn. Lehman explained that one bank was not enough. That Wall Street banks like to travel in packs. They said my thesis would only work if a couple of their peers also invested. They suggested I call Marc Rosenthal at Morgan Stanley and Jose Marques at Credit Suisse. Lehman was only interested in BATS if I could get the other banks to invest alongside them. I left the meeting hopeful, but realized I still had a tough road ahead. We agreed to continue discussions.

The Call

As I was walking out of Lehman, I got a call from Joe Ratterman. "Are you sitting down?" he asked. "No," I replied. "Well, you might want to sit down", he said somberly.

I sat down on Lehman's front steps. In a dark-blue suit with a red tie, I looked out of place sitting on the steps. All kinds of people hurriedly passed by on the sidewalk in front of me.

BATS trading volume had picked up. Joe explained that the accounting team had updated some calculations, taking into account the higher volume. "Bad news – we will violate our net capital requirement on Monday at current volume levels. What do you want me to do?"

"Let me call you back in ten minutes, " I said stunned. My head was spinning. I just sat there on the front steps of Lehman, almost in tears, and pondered. Should I give up?

Then suddenly, I had an idea. I could save BATS if I invested an additional $2 million. That was a significant portion of my liquid net worth at the time. I called my wife and calmly explained the situation. "Do what you think is best," Jamie said. My wife is always the more cautious one in our relationship, so I was surprised by how quickly she got on board.

Then, I called Dan Tierney at Getco and explained the predicament. He said it was fine if I wanted to invest. At this key juncture, Dan's support gave me the confidence to proceed.

I called back Joe. "You will get a wire tomorrow." Joe was stunned.

The additional $2 million investment was made at $4 per share. It was done on the same terms I was pitching to Lehman. With the additional money from me, I figured we now had only about 45 days to raise additional capital. The pressure was on.

Morgan Stanley and Credit Suisse

The next day, I had a meeting with Marc Rosenthal at Morgan Stanley. Morgan Stanley's office was about two blocks from Lehman's. I also scheduled a meeting with Jose Marques from Credit Suisse.

Both Marc and Jose are nice guys. They are engineers at heart and were deeply involved in trading and electronic trading systems. It was easy to speak to them. They got it. They saw how electronic trading was rapidly changing the business. Both had heard about BATS and convinced their firms to connect. They knew BATS had great technology and a friendly team.

Even though Marc and Jose got it, they each worked in a much larger organization. Each big bank contains a variety of personalities, viewpoints, and competing agendas. They could get me the meetings, but they could not stick their necks out too far without the support of their respective teams.

"Who the f*** are you and why are you wasting my time?" was the greeting I received when I first pitched the BATS investment to the senior people at Morgan Stanley. "Just give me a minute. My firm, Tradebot, trades more shares per day than Morgan Stanley." That instantly got their attention. They were blown away that a small firm in Kansas City that they had never heard of could be responsible for so much volume. We had a good hour-long meeting. They asked more tough questions.

I had two meetings at Credit Suisse. The meeting with the electronic trading group went well. The group was headed by Dan Mathisson. In 1999, the same year I started Tradebot, Dan joined Credit Suisse and launched an algorithmic brokerage business called AES. It was quite innovative at the time. One of their early customers happened to be

American Century in Kansas City.

My second meeting was with their investment team, headed by Alan Freudenstein. Let's just say Alan has a bit more of an abrasive personality. Over the years I have developed a deep respect for Alan's business knowledge. He is one of the shrewdest investors I have known.

Tower
I also stopped by to see Peter Buckley at Tower. Peter was in charge of business development. His boss, Mark Gorton, and a few other partners owned Tower (a hedge fund) and Lime Brokerage. They were two separate companies but had overlapping ownership. Peter recommended to Mark that they make an investment in BATS.

Mark scratched his head, and then disappeared from the room. In a few minutes, he came back with an email I had sent him from 2001 asking if they wanted to provide retail brokerage for Tradebot. I had completely forgotten that I had sent it. Mark quickly concluded, "I'm in for two." He turned to one of his partners, "You want two?" His partner said yes. I was completely blown away by how quick they moved. Subject to due diligence, they had just committed $4 million like it was sandwich money. The whole conversation lasted less than an hour.

Goal Line
Within a month, Lehman, Morgan Stanley, Credit Suisse, and Lime/Tower closed the deal and became BATS investors at $4 per share. To be more precise, Marc Rosenthal pointed out it was exactly 29 days from our first meeting to BATS receiving their wire. Marc said it was the fastest he had ever seen Morgan Stanley make an investment.

For due diligence, each big bank had their process. A long list of documents, forms, and financials was required for review. Basically, we put every contract and every official document we had on a zip drive and overnighted it to them. They were impressed with how quickly we could get them accurate data. They flew out to our offices in Kansas City to meet the rest of my team. They were impressed we only spent $24 a foot on our nice office space, since good space in New York costs much more. We had a meeting in our conference room overlooking the Kansas

116

City skyline. As luck would have it, there was an airshow scheduled for the next day. During warm-up exercises, the Blue Angels buzzed our building. They joked, "How did you arrange that?"

Each firm (especially Lehman, Morgan, and CS) only wanted in if the others were also in. Together, they knew BATS would be the winning table, and they each wanted a seat. With our new investors, we now had the money and the alliances we needed to succeed. Existing investors, including me, got significantly diluted, but our future was starting to look much brighter. I now owned a smaller piece of a much larger pie.

After the round closed, Mike Bleich took me aside. He said everyone was on the fence at first. He told me that my additional $2 million investment changed their perception of BATS. He said, "On Wall Street, there are droves of people who want others to take all the risk. With BATS, you were willing to put your own money on the line first."

At the time, my additional $2 million investment was extremely risky. In hindsight, it proved to be the turning point that put BATS on the road to success. It was not easy. It was stressful. We did what we had to in order to score. We got the ball over the goal line.

Momentum
In a lot of situations, it is all about momentum. Breaking the inertia of the status quo is difficult. A body at rest stays at rest.

A body in motion stays in motion. When the industry heard about the investments, they knew BATS was for real. Brokerage and trading firms now took us seriously. Many firms raised the priority of connecting to BATS. Our volume slowly climbed as more and more firms got connected.

Having three big Wall Street banks as investors changed many perceptions. BATS became acceptable to the insiders.

Elevator Pitch
Every good founder should have a good 'elevator pitch'.

This is a true story. I was at Morgan Stanley's office with Marc Rosenthal. We entered the elevator on the ground floor. We stopped on the fourth floor and on walked John Mack, the legendary CEO of Morgan Stanley. Marc did not waste the opportunity, "Mr. Mack. This is Dave Cummings. Morgan just made an investment in BATS, a new stock market that Dave founded." I briefly described our mission to provide competition to Nasdaq and NYSE. Mr. Mack appeared pleased, "I wish you the best of luck." He shook my hand as he stepped off the elevator. Marc and I rode on up. He said relieved, "I'm sure glad that went well."

The Bull

Merrill Lynch, Pierce, Fenner & Smith traced its roots to 1914. Over the years, they rose to prominence on the strength of their brokerage network, sometimes referred to as the 'thundering herd'. A bull was their logo.

The guys at Lehman introduced me to Mike Stewart at Merrill. They were good friends. One day, I walked into Merrill's offices in lower Manhattan and asked for Mike Stewart. "You will have to be more specific, we have four Mike Stewart's in this building," said the gal at the security desk. Once we found the right Mike, things went smoothly.

Merrill made an investment in BATS in late 2006 at $7 per share.

As BATS grew we kept expanding our circle of investors. As long as each firm held enough shares, they each got a seat on the BATS Board of Directors. In addition to the board seat, each firm also had the right to appoint a non-voting advisor. As BATS grew, more and more people came to our board meetings. Making room at the table was a key to our success.

The Bear

Not every big bank got to invest in BATS.

Brett Redfearn was a former American Stock Exchange executive who worked on electronic trading at Bear Stearns. While he was at the AMEX, he saw volume shift out of their SPY pit and onto the screens at Island and Arca. He knew electronic trading was the wave of the future. There are a small handful of people on Wall Street who really get the intricacies of market structure, and Brett is one of them. He suggested

Bear should make an investment in BATS. Bear came out to Kansas City for due diligence.

A couple weeks later, I dropped by Bear Sterns headquarters in New York. I liked working with Brett. On the other hand, one of his bosses, who shall remain nameless, was a complete asshole. He had a huge ego. He looked down his nose at us. He just rubbed me the wrong way. So, I told Brett I was refusing to take money from Bear. Brett relayed the message up the chain. "Uh, he wants to speak to you. It might get a little tense," Brett warned. From my pit trading days, I had developed a pretty thick skin, so I was not too worried as I walked down to the boss's corner office.

My skin got an inch thicker that day. "Who the hell do you think you are? No one turns down money from Bear. I will see to it that your name is black-balled up and down the street." Then, he got right in my face and just exploded uttering a rash of four letter words.

In the trading pits, you learn not to back down from a confrontation. "Well, go f*** yourself. And when you are done, you can shove the rest of Bear Stearns up your ass," I yelled back in his face even louder. He looked stunned. He was not the type of person who expected you to fight back. I stormed out. It was definitely a tense meeting.

Bear Stearns had a reputation for playing hardball. I do not regret for one minute turning him down. You get one jerk in the room and the whole tone of the conversation changes. Most of Wall Street is not like that anymore, but unfortunately there are still a few bad apples.

I was not sad to see Bear Stearns crash and burn in March 2008.

The ashes of Bear got picked up by J.P. Morgan. JPM is a much better place. Sometimes, there are great people in bad organizations. I still have a good relationship with Brett. He now holds a similar role as an electronic trading expert at JPM.

NYC

I have always had a love-hate relationship with Wall Street and New York City in particular. On one hand, my chosen career has allowed me to meet many good people at many firms around the Big Apple. I have made a number of friends.

On the other hand, being from Kansas City, I never felt like a part of the Wall Street inner circle. I like my place in life. I enjoy visiting New York for three or four days. Then, it wears on me. I am ready to escape, to get away from the traffic and the noise. I know Wall Street, but I am not part of Wall Street.

Three Wise Men
In addition to my contacts at the big banks, I have met many good people at smaller firms. The book is too short to mention everyone, but let me highlight three gentlemen I have known each for over ten years.

Richard Repetto is the longest-serving financial analyst in the sector. He works for the boutique investment bank Sandler O'Neill. Rich is a West Point graduate. His support for this country and our veterans is amazing. From the first time I met Rich, I just knew this was a guy I could trust. Rich has relationships with many of the buy-side asset managers, both large and small. In the early days of BATS, Rich hosted a dinner. I got to speak to the buy side about what BATS was up to and how we would disrupt Nasdaq.

Larry Tabb runs TABB Group, a research and strategic advisory firm focused exclusively on capital markets. Larry is a trusted voice in the industry. The TABB group has an online website called The Tabb Forum which features an honest debate about market structure from many thoughtful points of view. Many in this industry are quick to advocate changes that would help their business at the expense of their competitors. I have always respected Larry and his firm for keeping a thoughtful, neutral, and balanced perspective.

Richard Rosenblatt is the founder of Rosenblatt Securities. Rosenblatt is one of the few old-school NYSE floor brokers that made the pivot to remain relevant in the new world of electronic trading. Richard is a living textbook of NYSE history and the debates behind the rule changes. You must understand history to better understand where we are headed.

Rosenblatt and Sandler O'Neill both host a conference every year. Some years, they invite me to speak on a panel. Some years, they just invite me to hang out and mingle. I always seem to run into Larry Tabb. In my opinion, these two conferences are the best in the industry. I have been attending both for nearly a decade now.

The January Effect

It was December 2006. BATS had been open for business less than one year. We put up our first 100 million share trading day. I sent out an email to the industry boasting that we would have a billion share day by the end of our second year. Most people thought I was completely insane.

By this time, most of the major firms had completed their connections to BATS, yet our volume was still small compared to Nasdaq. I knew our ownership group controlled close to half of all the order flow on the street, but there was just one problem: we needed them and the rest of the industry to all hit the gas at the same time.

I presented a crazy idea to the board that I called 'The January Effect'. Our business was going to bleed a couple million a year for the next several years if we waited for the volume to slowly ramp up at the normal pace. What if we inverted our prices and actually paid firms to trade on BATS. We budgeted about $4 million for the January 2007 promotion. Marc Rosenthal at Morgan Stanley called it either the boldest thing or the stupidest thing he had ever heard. "Let's try it," he said, and the rest of the board went along with the proposal.

I sent out my email to the industry announcing BATS planned to lose $4 million in January. Boy did it provoke a response! Half the people thought it was brilliant, the other half thought I was completely nuts.

Bob Greifield made a comment to the analysts about "unsustainable business models". I publicly asked whether he meant ours or his. I explained that spending $1.16 billion to buy out Inet and Brut was stupid if I could recreate a market for less than $30 million.

The Winning Table

'The January Effect' worked. BATS volume skyrocketed to over 300 million shares per day. What most people forget is that our volume also grew in February, the month after we removed the inverted pricing

121

stimulus. With a network-effects business, it's all about the momentum.

Wall Street usually sides with the winner. At BATS, we continued to build our coalition. We added investments from Citibank, JP Morgan, and Deutsche Bank. Jose Marques had moved from Credit Suisse to Deutsche Bank. Jose likes to point out that he was the only person that got not just one, but two big banks to invest in BATS.

Each time we added an investor, we added another chair around the board room. Our investor group included three top trading firms (Tradebot, Getco, and Tower), a top clearing firm (Wedbush), and seven of the top ten investment banks (Lehman, Morgan, Credit Suisse, Merrill, Citi, JPM, and Deutsche Bank).

Beginning with my initial seed investment in June 2005 through the end of 2007, BATS raised over $150 million in capital. Investment rounds were priced at $1.00, $3.00, $4.00, $7.00, $15.00, and $25.00 per share.

Unwanted Suitor

In early 2007, Nasdaq launched a hostile takeover for the London Stock Exchange (LSE). Many in the British press were not too happy about the situation. Somehow, the British press had received my forwarded emails and were looking to write about anything that was anti-Nasdaq. One elderly tabloid reporter called me and we had a chat. "Never since the Germans bombed us in World War 2 have we felt so insulted as a nation," she said with a dry British humor. "What does this Yankee Bob Greifeld think he is up to?" The British are very proud of their market. The London Stock exchange can trace its roots back more than 300 years. For longer than America has been a country, they have been trading stocks in London.

The LSE was run by a stately lady named Clara Furse. Though I never met her in person, we chatted by phone a few times. I sent her a box with a BATS-logo baseball bat. On the bat I placed a handwritten yellow post-it note with the words, "This will help you beat back your unwanted suitor".

She called me upon receipt of the package. "You must come to London and meet me for tea." Sadly, I never got a chance to take Ms. Furse up on her offer.

On February 10, 2007 it became clear that Nasdaq's $5.3 billion hostile bid for the LSE had failed. They had only been able to buy about 28.75% of the shares rather than the 50% they needed to gain control.

"Bob the Bully" was the subject of an email I sent out, mocking Nasdaq's CEO, Robert Greifeld. I totally ripped into Bob and the pompous nature of the take-over battle. By far, that email provoked the most email responses. Some could not agree more, Nasdaq was out of line. Others, including a couple on my board, believed my criticism had gone too far and was unprofessional.

I wanted to crush Nasdaq in their moment of pain. A couple board members called me and said in no uncertain terms that Nasdaq's pain would not be good for the industry or their business. We could compete, but we needed to 'play nice'. I sarcastically asked Joe Ratterman if it was time for a grown up to run this business.

11. The Decision

You never get to live life twice. There are times when you reach a major fork in the road. You choose your path, and you move ahead.

You never get to go back. However, years later you may look back and ponder what a different choice could have brought. Would it have been more fun? Would you have encountered setbacks? You will never know. You never get to live twice.

BATS Expansion

By mid-2007, BATS was clearly on a strong growth path. Less than two years from incorporation, and less than eighteen months from product launch, we had gone from an idea to a high of 399 million shares matched in a single day. Up and down the street, most firms were connected to BATS. With significant capital raised from our investors, we had a strong balance sheet.

The BATS brand stood for disruptive innovation. We were well known in the industry and starting to become known among the general public. It is not easy to take on established network-effects businesses like Nasdaq and NYSE. We were really doing pretty well. We were approaching 10% market share, but we were not done. Each quarter, our volume continued to grow.

Having established a foothold in America, our board was urging BATS to expand into Europe. I wondered if we would expand too quickly and get over extended. Getting things up and running in London would take quite an effort. There would be increased risk. I was not looking forward to additional travel and more time away from home.

In America, BATS began filling out our exchange application with the SEC. It was time for BATS to become a full-fledged stock exchange. An ECN and a stock exchange do essentially the same thing, but have significantly different regulatory structures. Some of the operations are different as well. I will not dive into these differences in this book. Call someone in the industry or the SEC if you want to learn more.

The Dilemma

Everyone in the industry knew I owned Tradebot (a broker-dealer). I was also the CEO of BATS. From an operational perspective, everything was fine. There was a 'Chinese Wall' between Tradebot and BATS. The firms were in separate buildings. Except for myself, the firms had all separate people, and I did not take a day-to-day operational role within Tradebot. In the early days, we got several questions from customers and investors about the effectiveness of the 'Chinese Wall'. Those who looked into it came to the conclusion that the separation between Tradebot and BATS was real. These were two different firms.

The SEC had a rule that no executive of an exchange could own a controlling interest in a broker-dealer. Since the next logical step for BATS was to become a full-fledged stock exchange, I faced a major dilemma. I either needed to sell Tradebot or leave BATS.

Where's the Next Getco?

On April 13, 2007 the Wall Street Journal reported that Getco had received an investment from General Atlantic that valued Getco at $1.5 billion ($300 million for 20%). Aaron Lucchetti was the author. He was the same reporter who had previously covered me.

Getco was advised on the deal by the boutique investment bank Keefe, Bruyette, & Woods. The deal had been widely shopped around. Everyone was talking about it. Some were surprised by how big Getco had become. A few were surprised by the valuation. The deal confirmed what many had been seeing, that electronic trading was on the rise.

Wall Street tends to run as a pack. Among private equity, General Atlantic is considered by many to be 'smart money'. If they were placing a bet on an electronic trading firm, maybe there was money to be made in this new sector. Many of the private equity firms and investment banks started looking to make investments in Getco's competitors.

Around the industry, Tradebot was becoming fairly well-known. I had spoken on a number of industry panels. I started receiving calls from potential investors. "Was Tradebot the next Getco?" was the essence of each inquiry. I often heard, "Is Tradebot looking for a private equity investment?" or "Is Tradebot for sale?"

I really hadn't planned on selling Tradebot, but I took the calls anyway. When Wall Street is throwing money around, it never hurts to listen to the pitch.

Jerry Donini from Lehman approached me about the possibility of buying Tradebot. For the right price, I said I would consider it. We signed an exclusivity agreement. The Lehman team did full due-diligence on Tradebot and was impressed.

Mike Bleich explained that Lehman often looked up to Goldman Sachs and Morgan Stanley. Both were more advanced than Lehman in proprietary trading. Trading was, is, and always will be, an arms race. Mike jokingly summed up the situation like this, "Our customers have sticks and stones. We have pistols. Goldman has machine guns. Then holy shit, Tradebot and Getco show up out of nowhere with nuclear weapons." Wall Street never wants to be out-gunned. Since they were behind in the arms race, Lehman wanted to make the investment needed to catch up.

Lehman sent me a written offer to acquire Tradebot for $160 million. However, there was an unexpected twist. The purchase price was not in cash, it was 100% in Lehman stock. If I took the deal, it would have made me Lehman's largest individual shareholder.

The Decision

It was a lot of money, $160 million dollars. Of course, I discussed it with my wife. She was not fond of selling to Lehman, but wanted it to be my decision.

I spoke to Rob Alumbaugh. He told me that he personally did not really want Tradebot to become a part of Lehman Brothers. He said, "But that's a lot of money, and I wouldn't blame you if you took the deal." He continued, "I agree with Lehman's thesis, expand Tradebot into more asset classes and countries, like Getco has done." He continued, "But what do we need Lehman for? Can't we just do this ourselves?"

Two Paths
My life had reached a major fork in the road. I spent the next three days
pondering what to do. One path was to sell Tradebot and remain CEO at
BATS. BATS was expanding rapidly and would soon start a push into
Europe. BATS gave me a bigger platform and a chance to become more
well-known.

Down the other path, I could resign from BATS and return to Tradebot.
While I was gone, automated trading had grown rapidly. I was curious
to see if our business could reach new heights. I was an engineer at
heart, and electronic trading was the ultimate puzzle.

Both paths were interesting, but one provided me more control of my
destiny. At Tradebot, I owned the company. At BATS I was a
shareholder, but my job was to work for the board. I remembered Craig
Salvay's words from 1999, "Remember to be happy."

The following Monday, I turned down Lehman's offer.

The Path Not Taken
I will never know what my life would have been like if I had stayed at
BATS and taken Lehman's offer.

I do know that I dodged a major bullet that day. Seventeen months after
turning down their offer, on September 15, 2008, Lehman Brothers filed
for Chapter 11 bankruptcy. My shares in Lehman would have been
completely worthless.

After I turned down the Lehman offer, I knew my days at BATS were
limited. I just had to find the right time to make my exit.

Jumping Off
There is never a good time to jump off a fast moving train.

It was very clear to me that Joe Ratterman was the right man to succeed
me as BATS' CEO. He had been there from the beginning. He knew
how to run a larger organization. He even had some international
experience in a prior job. Most importantly, he had the full confidence
and support from our associates.

Even though I had full confidence in Joe, I was not too sure how the board felt about giving Joe the top job. He was soft-spoken, a classic 'inside' COO. At the time, most on the board probably did not view him as the right 'external face' for the organization.

I was afraid that if I allowed time for a typical succession plan, the board would select someone other than Joe. They would probably pick someone from New York who had 'experience running a market'. I have always valued talent more than experience. I knew Joe was right for the top job, if the board would just give him a chance.

With this in mind, I resigned abruptly from my CEO position on June 29, 2007. I told the board Joe would be in charge on an interim basis, effective "right now". In due time, the board decided to make Joe the permanent Chairman and CEO of BATS. Though no longer CEO, I remained on the board of directors.

The board was not too happy about my sudden departure. To make matters worse, I told the board Kelly Burkhart would also be going back to Tradebot. This made the board even more angry.

I had twisted Kelly's arm to help me when I started BATS. From our days together at Cerner, he had always been loyal to me. He wanted to follow me back to Tradebot, and I was going to make that happen, regardless of the board's opinion. Things between me and the board were tense for a few weeks.

My Last Word

After announcing my resignation to the board, I headed back to my office. I pushed the 'send' button on one final email to industry that I had composed. That email contained the following passage:

Reflections

In June 2005, I started BATS ECN to restore competition among market centers. Two years later, we have largely accomplished the original goal. Together, we have created the third largest equities market center – and we should be proud.

Running a market center is an once-in-a-lifetime opportunity and I thank you for your support throughout the process. Every morning I asked myself how we could take our 5 year plan and make it into a 1 year plan – this is running at BATS speed. I have no regrets.

Measuring a Founder
How do you measure the value of a company founder? I believe the true worth of a founder is properly measured after he is gone.

BATS was never about me. It was about building an organization with the right DNA to take on the establishment. It was about building a market that put the customer squarely in focus.

Over the next seven years, BATS continued to grow under Joe Ratterman's leadership. They launched a market in London, and started getting some early traction. In order to get critical mass quickly, they merged with a competitor, Chi-X Europe. After the European merger, BATS had the largest trading volume in Europe, eclipsing LSE and Deutsche Bourse.

To gain market share in American equities, BATS merged with Direct Edge, another upstart ECN. Going into the merger, BATS was number three, and Direct Edge was the number four market. Combined, they would surpass Nasdaq's volume.

BATS launched a stock options market that was also successful.

In less than a decade, we had gone from a scrappy startup to the number one market by volume in Europe and the number two market in the United States. BATS had become a multi-geography and multi-asset class exchange operator. Not bad for a group of outsiders from Kansas City.

Pass It On
By summer of 2014, the BATS Board of Directors was thinking about going public. Joe Ratterman had worked long hours for nine years. He

decided it was time to pass the baton to a new leader. That new leader would need to be comfortable as a public company CEO.

A short-list of candidates was drawn up. I was placed on the selection committee. Joe and I flew to New York to interview our top pick, Chris Concannon. After working at the SEC, Island, and Nasdaq, Chris had joined one of the leading high-frequency trading firms in New York, Virtu Financial. As I interviewed Chris, I knew he was the right person to take BATS to the next level. Joe and the rest of the board agreed. Chris became BATS' third CEO in Spring 2015.

After ten years of service, I stepped down from BATS Board of Directors in the summer of 2015. Though I had learned so much from the people around that table, I felt like it was time for me to move on.

IPO
BATS was a company that was always destined to go public. For BATS, that day was April 15, 2016. The post-split IPO shares were priced at $19.00 per share. The IPO was successful and the stock closed at $23.00 after the first day of trading. The IPO raised $252.7 million.

> *[Note: As a private company BATS paid a series of dividends totaling $25.74 per share. Right before going public, BATS split their stock 1 for 2.91.]*

A public company and a private company are very different. Different times call for different people in the seats. A public company director has a fiduciary responsibility to all shareholders. Most public companies avoid the appearance of conflicts of interest by having the majority of their boards comprised of independent directors.

Like me, several of BATS' long-time board members and advisors stepped off the board in preparation for the company going public.

To celebrate the successful IPO, BATS decided to gather many of the long-time board members, advisors, and the management team for one last dinner together. It was scheduled for Tuesday, July 12, 2016. I flew out to New York for the event.

A Key Stop Before Dinner

After landing around noon, I dropped by One Liberty Plaza to catch up with my old nemesis, Bob Greifeld, CEO of Nasdaq.

Three Nasdaq executives, Bob Greifeld, and I met for an hour. It was in the very same conference room that I had been in with Bob and Chris Concannon 11 years earlier. I purposefully sat in the same chair where Bob had wished me "Good luck with that."

Our meeting was cordial. We discussed the industry, how things had changed, and where things were headed. Bob congratulated me on the successful IPO at BATS. I apologized for picking on him in my emails to the industry. Today, Tradebot has a great relationship with Nasdaq and is one of its largest customers.

I had won. Yet strangely, Bob had not lost. He was still the head of Nasdaq, and Nasdaq was bigger and more profitable than they had been 11 years prior. The duopoly was gone, and in its place there were now three competing markets: NYSE, Nasdaq, and BATS.

No one could argue now. BATS was firmly part of the market structure establishment. It was surreal. In many ways, BATS had become what we were trying to disrupt.

Switching Teams

Chris Concannon was now running BATS. It is funny how good people sometimes switch teams, yet remain in the industry.

My meeting with Bob included Tal Cowen, who once ran Chi-X, and Tom Whitman, whom I had met in 2003 when he was at Philly. Both men were now Nasdaq executives.

After my meeting with the Nasdaq executives, I also met with Barry Nobel. I have known Barry since 2003 in Philly. He had recently announced he was leaving Nasdaq and retiring. We had a good, long heart-to-heart chat. Again, I hate to see good people leave our industry.

The Last Supper

I took a cab over to Sparks Steakhouse on 46th Street for supper.

Looking around the table, I knew it was the last time this group of people would dine together. It was truly an incredible collection of talent. Among us were about half of the top market structure experts in the business. Seven large investment banks and three key high-frequency trading firms were represented.

Since not everyone could attend the event, Joe Ratterman made sure to read off the names of all the BATS Board Members and advisors who had helped us along the way. His list included names like Kelly Burkhart, Dan Tierney, Steve Schuler, and Dan Mathisson. This great coalition had made BATS successful.

Joe thanked us all for coming together. At dinner that night, he shared five things that he believed were key to BATS success:

1. Keep it Simple at First
2. Move Quickly
3. Plan to Scale
4. Raise Capital in Stages
5. Get Attention

He then asked me to say a few words. The night concluded with remarks from Chris Concannon. I appreciate that Joe took the time to reflect upon our journey.

12. The BATS Playbook

In this chapter, I would like to expand on Joe Ratterman's remarks. I will share some takeaways and key themes which I believe helped BATS to succeed. Some ideas are BATS specific, and some may work in other businesses. For those who would like to skip ahead, my personal career saga resumes in Part Three.

I do not claim to have all the answers. Yet, I would like to think there is some wisdom that I can share in these next few pages.

1. Customer Focus
From the very beginning, BATS focused on the customer experience. Coming from Tradebot, we knew what it was like to be a customer. We built the best playing field we could.

We built a great product. We priced it extremely aggressively, especially at first.

We asked, "How can we give our customers the best possible deal?" rather than, "How can we make the most money this month?"

We did not look for 'gotcha' ways to trick the customer with add-on charges. We wrote the documents and the contracts in a simple, straightforward manner.

We were careful to build a level playing field that was fair to all participants. We treated all customers, large and small, with respect. Customers felt like we really wanted their business. We were willing to work hard to earn it. We returned phone calls.

We knew the importance of building a trading system that was robust and that would not crash when the market got busy.

When we had a small glitch, we admitted our mistake and told the customers what actions we were taking to correct the problem.

2. Copy What Works

I proudly admit that we successfully copied the best features from Island, Archipelago, and others. We did not try to fix what was not broken. We used industry standard protocols. Our product documentation was modeled after theirs. We drafted our contracts using theirs as a reference. Our website was designed by asking what elements we liked from other sites.

It is important, I believe, to pull inspiration from more than one source. Copy what you like best about each business and try to ignore or eliminate the rest. No business is perfect. Start with the best ideas from your competitive niche, and then layer on top ideas from outside of your industry.

3. Start Simple

Our business model was extremely simple, especially at first. Basic limit order matching of buyers and sellers is the core feature of every electronic market. We got that up and running before we tried to add more complex features like routing orders to other markets.

We launched our product seven months after incorporation. In our space, that is very quick. There are many things you can only learn after going live with real-world customers. Start simple. Collect feedback.

4. Great Technology

People who know BATS know we built the system with world class technology. I have Kelly Burkhart, Paul Rose, Chris Isaacson, and Ken Conklin to thank for that. From the beginning, they designed a solid architecture that allowed the business to scale to millions of transactions without getting slow. This was not easy.

It's extremely hard to find and nurture great software developers. We never looked at our tech team as a 'cost center'. Rather, we looked at it as the place where we built our competitive advantage. Joe and I both had software development backgrounds. It makes a difference when senior management really understands developers and speaks their language. BATS was built by engineers, not lawyers.

5. Free Data

When I was CEO of BATS, we never charged for market data. Our free real-time quotes were even carried on Yahoo Finance. Giving away free data sent the message that we are all about transparency and analytics.

Free real-time data builds public confidence and trust in the market. This is so important. For its long-term survival, Wall Street needs to find a way to reach out and convert more Americans to investors. If the investor-class gets too small, there is a real risk that the politicians will turn against free-market capitalism.

Sadly, after I stepped down as CEO, BATS decided to start charging for its real-time market data like its competitors do. There is nothing illegal about this, but I still don't like the policy. Free the data and charge for the trades.

Outside our sector, you see several online businesses that got huge by giving away free information and data. Google, Facebook, and YouTube are good examples. Unlike physical goods, it costs almost nothing to copy and distribute data.

6. Network-Effect Business

The phone system is a classic example of a network-effect business. Every phone on the network becomes more valuable each time a new phone is added to the network. The value does not grow linearly, it grows exponentially.

Electronic exchanges are good examples of network-effect businesses. Every buyer wants to find more sellers, and vice-versa.

The value of a small network is low. It is very hard to get a network-effect business started. You have to 'Go Big or Go Home'. However, once you get a network-effect business to critical mass, it creates tremendous shareholder value. Once you get big, it gets almost hard to screw it up, unless you do something to hurt your customers.

7. Lower Switching Costs

In any business, you should carefully consider a customer's true 'switching cost'. Sometimes this is an intangible cost like building trust in your brand. In other cases, switching costs are real, like the cost of paying engineers to write an interface to your matching engine.

Once a customer gets past the initial switch, the ongoing cost of keeping them drops greatly as long as you are providing them value.

Knowing this, BATS did everything possible to lower switching costs. We intentionally started a very aggressive price war. We used standard protocols. We located in the same data center as Archipelago so that our customers would not need to order new data lines.

Conversely, anything that requires your new customers to change their workflow is a non-starter. A truly revolutionary product comes along rarely. For most products, the goal is to give customers what they are used to from competitors, plus a little something extra that justifies the cost of switching.

8. The Unbelievable Offer
Sometimes a great product at a great price is just not enough. BATS offered 'The January Effect' where we gave ridiculously aggressive prices to customers for a limited time in order to get them over the initial hump of connecting.

As I said in a previous chapter, critics looked at the short-run and said this was crazy. We considered the long-term shareholder value that would be created by getting to critical mass with a network-effect business. In this context, our unbelievable offer was 'crazy like a fox.'

9. Scalability
BATS makes a small amount per transaction across millions of tiny transactions per day. If you look at many big technology companies, their core business model falls into this category. If you aspire to make huge amounts of money, look for a highly-scalable business.

However, let me warn you that you will not be alone. The more scalable a business is, usually the more competitive it is. Building a technology business is hard. Taking on Wall Street is really hard.

Consider driving a cab. Your odds of making a decent living are higher, but your odds of becoming a millionaire are much lower. Driving a taxi is not scalable, but creating Uber is. Scalable businesses are almost always extremely competitive.

10. Branding

A company name is the shell into which a company matures.

BATS was a name that served us well. It denotes strength and aggressiveness.

Often using a baseball theme, our marketing efforts supported this image. We were always on offense. We were not afraid to take a swing. The full-size wooden baseball bats we sent out were a reminder to our competitors that their customer was now working with us.

The average person needs to hear a company name at least seven times before they consider it familiar. A big part of marketing is just getting your name in front of customers over and over.

The BATS theme worked for us. Pick what works for you.

11. Get Attention

Controversy gets attention.

My emails to industry got attention for BATS. Creating a controversy got people talking. I got to speak on industry panels. I got coverage in the press. The media always loves the underdog.

I was not afraid to make fun of Nasdaq in general and at its CEO Bob Greifeld in particular. I would never pick on 'a little guy' but Bob was not 'a little guy', he was the establishment and was fully capable of defending himself against my jabs.

Personalizing the imagery makes it more memorable. I would pose for pictures with a baseball bat. We were going to beat the crap out of Nasdaq. That was the message we wanted people to hear.

BATS stood for something. We were on a mission. We had a reason to exist – we were out to attack Nasdaq and challenge the status quo.

Too many companies are boring. They struggle to get noticed. As a startup, you can afford to be more edgy.

On the other hand, as a company gets larger, people naturally expect it to be more stable and more predictable. At the proper time, BATS made the pivot. I stepped down and Joe Ratterman stepped in. The company got more 'corporate' in its image. The messaging was still aggressive, but it was toned down a notch.

The best media strategy depends on the stage of a company. When you are bigger, keep it professional. When you are small, get attention.

12. Ask for the Sale
We did not wait for things to happen, we made things happen.

As the startup CEO, it was important for me to personally get out and get in front of real customers. An hour-long meeting face-to-face is usually what it takes to really get to know someone. Once the personal connection is made, emails and phone calls are given a higher priority.

In the early days, Kenny and I traveled to meet our customers face-to-face. We visited their offices. We asked for the sale. We listened to their feedback and adapted our product offering.

I should point out that not every customer was enthusiastic to see us. Many were skeptical at first. We did not stop with 'no'. We kept calling firms until we convinced them to connect to BATS and do business with us.

Of course, I could not know every customer. However, I had several key customers that I knew very well. My personal connections were a good representative sample of the industry. My job was to get the key customers on board. Our approach was different than our competitors. It was personal.

Over time BATS built a sales team and a more traditional structured process. This is what people expect of a more mature firm.

But in the early days, do not be structured. Be personal. Ask for the sale.

13. Exponential Capital
The money was tight in the early innings. This was a good thing.

BATS learned to be frugal. Having a tight budget made us focus on what was important to get to the next stage. As we hit milestones, we were able to raise more money at higher and higher valuations.

Each round was like a new level. We had to win at the small level before we could unlock more resources. In the early days, we had to get a lot done with a relatively small staff. As we raised capital, we were able to expand our team. We moved extremely quickly, but it still took some time for the team to gel, for the product to mature, and for the company to be ready to play at the higher levels.

In Silicon Valley and New York, I often hear about companies with too much money too early. If being frugal is not in a firm's early DNA, it is almost impossible to establish that discipline later.

However, once our business model was proven, we piled on huge amounts of capital at escalating valuations. When the momentum is in your favor, do not go slow. Huge returns are possible if you can quickly raise money at higher and higher valuations.

Our private investment rounds were priced at $1, $3, $4, $7, $15, and $25. Hitting our milestones proved the value of our business was increasing. In all, we raised more than $150 million in our first 30 months. Our shareholders received a tremendous rate-of-return, especially for our earliest investors who took the most risk.

14. Strategic Investors

Some businesses can bootstrap and do not need investors. For everyone else, you should carefully consider who you want around your table.

In many cases, customers or key vendors make very good early stage investors. Because their interest is strategic, rather than just financial, they often have a longer-term perspective. More importantly, they know your industry. They understand at a much finer level of detail what customers truly value. Many times, they know the strengths and weaknesses of your competitors and their products.

Every good CEO is made better by a strong board that thoughtfully challenges them and asks the tough questions. The BATS board took me outside my comfort zone. My two years as CEO and ten years on the board taught me invaluable life lessons.

By the way, some CEOs intentionally pack their boards with yes-men that politely agree with everything. If you want to be secure and mediocre, this is probably a good game plan. Too many public company boards are full of dopes with impressive resumes that are old, tired, and uninspiring. They are 'perfect fiduciaries,' trained to avoid risk at every opportunity. This results in a business that slowly hardens into a mind-numbing, dumbed-down bureaucracy. Every difficult decision requires a committee or an outside 'expert' consultant. Shortly before they leave, these drones will recommend that your firm sell-out to your competitor so their vested stock options can get one final hike in value (If you haven't noticed, I can be brutally honest at times).

This was not the approach we took with BATS. My board was never afraid to challenge me.

15. Land of Opportunity
America is the land of opportunity.

For BATS, I probably traveled from Kansas City to New York at least fifty times. I often landed at LaGuardia and took a taxi from Queens to Manhattan. "Where are you from?" I asked each cab driver. Almost all were born in far-away countries. "Why did you come to America?" Every cabbie had a fascinating story. I listened so carefully that I usually did not notice when we were stuck in traffic. In every case, they were so proud to be in America. Many wanted to make money so they could send it back home. Maybe someday the rest of their family could move here. For the price of a cab ride, each story was amazing.

Sadly, too many Americans that grow up here take this country for granted. If you need a reminder of how lucky you are, jump in a cab.

16. Halfway to India Strategy
One time, I joked that Kansas City was the "Halfway to India Strategy".

Around the time I was starting BATS, outsourcing IT jobs to India was a key theme around Wall Street. Many big firms laid off droves of their tech team and replaced them with cheaper labor in Mumbai.

Too many people on the coasts do not realize what great tech talent we have in what they derisively call "Flyover Country". The cost of living in the Midwest is so much lower than Manhattan or Silicon Valley. Rather than outsource halfway around the world, why not move more jobs to the heartland? We are one time zone away from New York. We too have high-speed internet access. We read the same news. Our state universities turn out great engineering talent.

For BATS, I believe it was a key competitive advantage to have our programmers and accountants in Kansas City. There are some roles, like sales, that are outward facing. These jobs, I have to admit, are probably more effective in New York. But for the inward facing jobs, why locate people in the high-rent district?

17. Honest People
Our firm was full of honest, straightforward people.

We hired people who were decent and hardworking. They followed the golden rule and treated others like they wanted to be treated.

Maybe this sounds too simplistic, but believe me, it really works. Either people trust you or they don't. It does not appear on the balance sheet, but it does make all the difference in the world.

18. Organic First
As an engineer, I like to build things.

There is a pride and joy that comes from building a firm. There is a satisfaction that comes from delivering a good product. These intrinsic motivations are often more powerful than money.

Nasdaq and NYSE acquired much of the technology at the core of their matching engines. We built ours from scratch. When you build something, there is an increased pride of ownership.

To me, the most exciting stages of a company are when it experiences a high rate of organic growth.

As a company gets larger, it gets harder and harder 'to move the needle' with organic growth. Most larger firms turn to acquisitions to supplement their internal growth. This is not inherently good or bad, it is just the natural lifecycle of a startup that becomes a large firm. Once a firm is large, it's difficult for its leaders to carve out the time for deep engineering work. It's easier to manage a large span-of-control with a focus on budgets and deals.

This is the path BATS took. Joe Ratterman and I are engineers, and Chris Concannon is an attorney.

Engineers come early, and lawyers come later. It is just the way the world works.

19. Accelerate Time

"Let's do the time warp again." Great line from the classic film, *The Rocky Horror Picture Show*.

At BATS, we tried to imagine where we wanted to be in five years. Then, we raced to accomplish as much of that agenda as possible in one year. Every year, we reset our goals and started the sprint again.

"It is all about momentum". I would often repeat this phrase around the halls of BATS. Especially in the early stages of a company, it's often easier to climb a hill if you take an aggressive run at it rather than a leisurely pace.

Payroll is the biggest cost item at many firms. You have to pay well in order to get the best people. Do not be cheap with your people. Rather, be frugal by getting more done in less time.

20. Celebrate Milestones

Don't be afraid to lay out big, hairy, audacious goals.

At BATS, we set extremely aggressive, almost ridiculous, goals for ourselves. One hundred million shares matched in a day, a billion shares matched, and having the fastest matching engine in the industry were some of our goals.

We hit them. Then, we paused for a moment to reflect and celebrate as a team. Launching a company takes a great deal of hard work from many people. Remember to take time to savor the victories along the way.

I did not allow alcohol in our office, so Joe Ratterman started a tradition at BATS of buying ice cream bars for everyone when we hit a milestone.

I would rather hit a high goal one month late than step over a low bar without breaking a sweat. In too many companies, management teams play the game of lowering expectations so that it will be easier 'to beat their numbers'. I do not do this. Maybe that's why I've never been a good middle manager in corporate America.

21. Play to Win

Yes, there is a difference between leaving the ball on the one yard line and getting it over the goal line.

Winning matters. Winning is different from losing. As a leader, it is so important to define what winning means for your team. Over time, the definition of winning changes.

We tended to hire people who were naturally competitive. I often used analogies from sports. "Winning is not everything, it's the only thing." This was my favorite line from legendary Green Bay Packers coach Vince Lombardi.

22. Thick Skin

You can never please all of the people all of the time.

BATS fought a hard fight. I took some heat. It's just part of the game. Fighting Wall Street is not like kindergarten. Not everyone plays nice.

As a struggling upstart, it's not too hard to find some love. The bigger you get, the more people will get jealous. If you go far, you will get many arrows in your back.

I developed a thick skin. I still listen to my thoughtful critics, because they often make a good point. They are fair, and I can learn from them.

On the other hand, there are always naysayers that hate you no matter what. They hate you because you have money and are successful. These are little people who will never go far in life with that attitude.

Unfortunately, there are a lot of envious people in this country. Many in the political arena have made a career out of demonizing 'the upper 1%'. I don't think it's going to get better, and it even seems to be getting worse. As a nation, if we do not celebrate success, we will not have as much success. Jealously does not lead to prosperity.

23. The Deep End
Do not be afraid to throw employees into the deep end.

BATS took a number of early-career associates and gave them tons of responsibility. I will not name names here because I do not want to leave anyone out. There were many young associates who rose to the challenge.

Sometimes, they made small mistakes, learned, and quickly changed course. This was expected. What was not expected was how quickly they grew and matured. They developed leadership skills. They earned the respect of their peers and the industry.

Never be afraid to throw a young superstar into the deep end. A few times, you will need to dive in to rescue them. More often than not, they will rise to the top.

24. Share Success
Spread those stock options around.

I would recommend this only in a company that plans to go public in the not-too-distant future. If a company plans to remain private, I believe a bonus pool is a better way to reward associates.

At BATS, all early associates were granted stock options. The options vested over a period of four years. The board established a pool of stock options and gave me discretionary authority as the CEO to make grants to associates as I thought appropriate.

Paul Rose was one of our key developers. He was on the quiet side, always worked hard, and came up with several clever solutions for our software architecture. People who know Paul know that he is a genius.

One day, I arrived at work before 7:00 a.m. On my way in, I saw Paul's yellow Mustang. I left after 6:00 p.m. Paul's yellow sports car was still in the spot next to mine.

The next day, I went into Joe Ratterman's office. I told him I was granting additional stock options to Paul. He had more than earned them, and I wanted to send a strong message that we valued our engineers.

Most times, we made grants at regular intervals to associates throughout the company. Occasionally, we made one-time exceptions. There was not a lot of bureaucracy, and we made sure to reward our best people.

When BATS went public, many of the early associates held options or stock worth a significant amount of money. The associates felt like owners, because they were owners.

25. Let Go

As a company founder, know when to get out of the way.

Most entrepreneurs have a very strong personality. It's one of the traits that makes us valuable. There are a number of venture backed companies where the founder hangs on too tight and the whole situation gets very weird. It is called the 'founder problem'.

It is important to realize that everyone has their strengths and their weaknesses. Few true entrepreneurs are happy or effective in a large organizations. It is hard for a founder to let go of 'their company'. But realize, if you take outside investment, it is not 'your company.' It belongs to the shareholders. From that point forward, it's not about creating the perfect dream job for yourself. It is about maximizing long-term shareholder return. In many cases, this requires hiring professional management once the organization starts to scale.

Each case is unique. In the case of BATS, it worked out perfectly. Because I did not 'need a job', I had the freedom to be a bit more edgy. My impatience created the momentum that gave BATS its competitive advantage. I doubt that I would have been as effective if I had toned it down and tried to stay for ten years. Joe Ratterman, on the other hand, would never have taken the risks that I took the first two years, but he was clearly the right leader for years three through ten.

26. Going Public

It takes a special type of company to go public.

Advisors generally do not recommend a company go public until it has at least a billion dollar market capitalization. In addition to size, the public markets generally prefer industries with relatively stable and predictable earnings.

The public market also expects companies to operate at a very high level of transparency, especially since the passage of Sarbanes-Oxley in 2002. Bottom line, being a public company executive is not as fun as it was before things got all legalistic.

As a stock exchange, BATS operates with a high level of regulatory oversight. The business model is easy to understand and highly scalable. Future earnings are reasonably predictable. Other companies in other industries are better off remaining private. I put most proprietary trading firms, like Tradebot, into this category.

BATS is the type of company that was destined to go public. It was well known, of sufficient size, and highly profitable.

Part Three

Return to Tradebot

13. Moving on Up

In July 2007, I returned to Tradebot. I had been gone for only 24 months to start BATS, but I returned as a much different person both personally and professionally. I was more confident. My management skills had developed. I was now well known in the industry.

A few months after returning to Tradebot, I sold about half of my BATS stock to Getco and Morgan Stanley for $28.8 million. I kept the other half of my BATS stock until after they went public. No matter what happened on the BATS side, I knew I had made a winning investment.

The Tradebot I returned to was a much different business than the one I had started on a shoestring out of a spare bedroom in 1999.

I had the rare opportunity to return to a business that I had founded after spending some time away. Tradebot was ready to grow.

Chairman
'Chairman of the Board' is the best job in the world. I once joked that my only responsibility was to have four board meetings a year. The rest I did, not because I had to, but because I wanted to. I am truly blessed. My job is my biggest hobby.

Chairman is a title I have held since starting Tradebot in 1999. It was a title I kept even while I was away at BATS, and the title I wanted upon my return. As Chairman, I see two main responsibilities:

1. To set the company vision and shape what we would become.
2. To hire the right associates and help guide the company culture.

Axis of Innovation
Even after my return, Rob Alumbaugh remained President and CEO of Tradebot. We talked at length about his role and mine. We made it clear to all associates that 'Rob ran the company.' He made the major decisions. He ran all day-to-day operations. He was responsible for the

profit and the losses. With Rob in charge, I had more time to focus on my pet projects.

I have the greatest respect for Rob. While I was away at BATS, he did an awesome job running the company and growing our trading profits. His small group of twenty people in Kansas City was starting to get some major traction, and I had to be careful not to get in his way.

Rob was amazingly productive. Not only was he the CEO, he also personally developed the code for 'the bot'. The bot was the most important piece of our trading system that held the logic that decided when to trade. Some of the logic was hardcoded, but much of it was driven by parameters. Rob realized this allowed the traders to adapt our trading strategies quickly as the market evolved.

In those days, the axis of innovation at Tradebot revolved around three associates: Rob Alumbaugh, Rich Stigall, and Eric Boles. Rich developed much of the order handling logic in the system. He also managed the other developers who worked on the quotes and the risk systems. Rich had a degree in Aerospace Engineering from the University of Missouri at Rolla. Early in his career, he had worked at Boeing, but for the last ten years or so he had focused on software development in C++.

Rich is known for being blunt. He does not sugar-coat things or tell you what you want to hear. He is flat out the most brutally honest person I have ever met. Many times, I would ask a question, and Rich's exact reply was "That would be stupid." It took a while for me to appreciate Rich's style. Once you get past the bluntness, you realize Rich is extremely smart, loves trading, and is a very productive developer. Rich also has a very strong Christian faith. He likes to run. One time, he won a 100 mile race. His blog about the experience makes it clear that his faith is what kept him going.

Eric Boles joined the firm as a trader in 2003 after the dot com implosion that put Biz Space out of business. His background had nothing to do with trading, but we hired him anyway. He was very bright, a critical thinker, but also had a sarcastic streak at times. Eric, with a graduate degree in Divinity from Yale, was the only Tradebot associate with an

Ivy League education. You would never know it from his demeanor. He grew up in the small southern Missouri town of Joplin. His dad was a professor at a religious school, College of the Ozarks.

Eric Boles was the Head of Trading. Managing all of the traders, his department was responsible for adjusting system parameters to maximize trading profits based on the market conditions each day. The traders also generated lots of ideas for system enhancements. Some ideas were good, and some were not so good.

Almost every day, you would find Rob, Rich, and Eric around a whiteboard discussing proposed enhancements to the trading system. It was an extremely quick iterative cycle. Priorities were set. New code was pushed out almost every week. Their innovation cycle was more nimble than our competitors, and we believed this gave us a significant advantage. There was little time for deep theory, the focus was on getting improvements into production. If things failed, the goal was to fail quickly and try something else next week. While I was away at BATS, the three of them made several key discoveries that resulted in much greater profits.

Kelly Burkhart also rejoined Tradebot after having spent two years with me at BATS. Kelly and Rich were both Vice Presidents of Software Development. Rich focused more on quotes and orders. Kelly focused on the database and the backend message handling infrastructure.

Kelly and Rich were always very respectful, but there were occasionally professional differences of opinion about our technical architecture. While Kelly and I were away at BATS, Tradebot had shifted most of its development to Microsoft Windows because that was the platform Rob and Rich preferred.

Kelly is a relentless Linux advocate. Little by little, he convinced Rich and Rob to convert more of our servers to the Linux operating system. Kelly is also a big advocate of open source. We use Postgres as our database rather than a proprietary system like Oracle. Over time, we've added other open source technologies like Python and Hadoop.

Expansion
In many ways, 2007 to 2010 was a very transformative time for Tradebot. We went in as a scrappy startup. We emerged a mid-size, well-capitalized firm.

Tradebot began 2007 with 20 associates. Over the next four years, our ranks swelled to around 70. Several of the key associates and leaders in our firm today joined us during this expansion period.

Rob and I had a vision of what we wanted the firm to become. The old 320 Armour building did not fit that vision. We needed a new space.

Briarcliff Hilltop
Briarcliff was expanding their business park again. Now under construction was their signature building – the Hilltop at Briarcliff. It was an eight story office tower on a hilltop overlooking downtown Kansas City.

Nathaniel Hagedorn had been my landlord for the BATS office space. His role within the Briarcliff Development Company continued to expand. Charles Garney, now in his seventies, had taken half-a-step back and was letting Nathaniel drive.

As Nathaniel pitched the project to me, I knew it would be the perfect place for our company. He took us up in a helicopter and we hovered at the elevation of the top floor. The view was amazing. Trains ran along the north bank of the Missouri River. The General Motors Fairfax car assembly plant was on the south side of the river. The downtown airport where my dad first worked for TWA was tucked into a river bend. The Kansas City skyline was the backdrop.

To me, it was not just a good view. It symbolized my place in life. Growing up in a suburb on the north side of KC, I could see the skyline of the city, but I was never a part of the downtown scene. It was the perfect blend of the suburbs and the city.

We signed a ten year lease for an entire floor. The floorplate was about 25,000 square feet, enough space to comfortably fit around 100 associates. We had no idea how large our firm would become headcount-wise, but I very much did not want to deal with running out of space and being jammed like we were in our old space. The floorplan was designed in a way that we could sublet some of our space if we did not need it. As it turned out, we occupied the entire floor.

Ron Schauwecker at Finkle Williams was the architect for our tenant finish. I made a rough sketch of how I wanted the floor laid out. Ron and Nathaniel took the basic concepts and gave us a design that was both functional and impressive. As you step off the elevator, there is a glass wall opening to our main reception area. Behind the reception area is a glass-walled conference room with the best view in Kansas City.

There is an interior classroom with enough space for the whole firm to get together for meetings. Clockwise around the outside of the floor are areas for the kitchen, finance team, two software development pods, the trade floor, the network team, and a third software development pod. The trade floor spans most of the north side of the building and overlooks the Briarcliff residential area.

Rob Alumbaugh, Kara Miller (my assistant at the time), and I reviewed plans and provided feedback during construction. I have no ability whatsoever to pick colors. Fortunately, Rob, Kara, and Nathaniel have a much better taste for aesthetics. The new space turned out great. I have been told by several people that Tradebot has the nicest offices in Kansas City.

Moving Day
We moved into our new space on August 22, 2008. After trading was finished at 3pm local time, everyone boxed up their stuff and crammed it into their cars. We hired movers for a few of the larger items.

By coincidence, Rob and I were two of the last people left at the old building. We made a final pass through the building, making sure we had not left anything behind. He reflected, "You know, we accomplished a lot together in this old building." He was right; the old building had served us well. After the move, we both knew Tradebot would no longer be a scrappy startup. That era of our existence was over and there was no going back.

Our new office is only 2.6 miles from the old one. We bought pizza for dinner and people stayed late to set up their new space. Several associates and some of their families came in Saturday to continue unpacking. There was a sense of excitement to be in the new space. Our firm had finally made enough money to afford a better space.

The servers and the network were the most critical components. The network team finished on Sunday. Everything ran smoothly when we opened for business the following Monday.

Grand Opening

A few weeks later, we held a grand opening to show off our new space to our friends and families. I asked our old landlord, Karl Morris from Concerned Care, to do the honor of cutting the ribbon. We put up a slide show showing pictures of Tradebot from the first nine years. We played the theme song from the television series The Jeffersons, "Movin' on Up".

The new facility is nice and has helped us greatly with our image. Yet, it is important that we always remember where we came from. We need to retain the DNA of a small, scrappy startup. As long as we think of ourselves as the underdogs, we will continue to keep winning.

First Impressions

First impressions matter more than most people think. Right or wrong, one forms a lasting impression about a business in the first five minutes of their first visit. Is this a serious business or a fly-by-night? Are the people friendly? Do they have their act together?

I underestimated the impact our new space would have on our ability to attract associates. Mysteriously, we found more meetings with vendors taking place at our office rather than us traveling to their office. Sometimes community groups or school groups would ask if they could drop by for a tour.

An expensive office is a waste of money for a company without a good business model and a good team. However, a suitable office space can accelerate the success of a firm with a solid core.

NYSE Visit

Duncan Niederauer and I first met when he was an executive at Goldman Sachs. I tried and tried to get Goldman as a BATS investor, but I was unable to close the deal with Duncan. Ultimately, Goldman decided instead to invest in BATS' competitor, DirectEdge.

Duncan became the CEO of the NYSE in 2007. In September of 2008, he requested a visit to Tradebot because we were becoming a significant customer of the NYSE. As we sat in our conference room overlooking the downtown KC skyline, he complimented me on what a nice space we had. I grinned. Inside my head, I thought back to the time I had been thrown out of the old NYSE after making a snide remark about their handhelds. Now the NYSE leader was coming to visit me. Times had changed.

I'm a bit of a smart-ass at times. I concluded my visit with Duncan by giving him a tour of our space. As we walked out onto our trading floor, I could not help but point out to Duncan that some days we did more trading volume on our floor than they did on the floor of the NYSE!

14. Canada & Beyond

Andy O'Hara is one of our traders. One day while we were having lunch, he asked, "Hey, why doesn't Tradebot expand into Europe?" "What about Canada," I shot back, "It's closer."

Andy had spent some time right out of college at the boutique investment bank of Lazard Freres. Unlike most people at Tradebot, Andy had genuine experience working for a Wall Street firm in Manhattan. After working at Lazard, Andy had moved back to his hometown, Kansas City. I met Andy when he was in his late twenties. He was working as a salesman for a local bank, and was referred to me by Nathaniel Hagedorn. Like many in banking sales, he held a VP title.

Andy visited Tradebot to try to sign us up as a customer with his bank. I explained to him that our banking was not too interesting because we didn't borrow money. Somehow in that conversation, he got more interested in trading than banking. We offered him a job and he went back and resigned. If any other young, smart bankers want to come looking for Tradebot's business, you know where to find us.

Many of our high-frequency competitors were working on European expansions (Getco had been in Europe since 2002). Up to this point, Tradebot conducted all of our business within the United States and Canada would be our first international expansion. We were eager to expand into more geographies and more asset classes.

Canadian Market Plans

When we looked closer, we realized what a great opportunity Canada might be. From Kansas City, Toronto was only two hours away and Air Canada had a direct flight. The securities industry in Canada is very tight-knit. Most of the major players have offices within about a five square block area in the heart of downtown Toronto. The Canadians we met were very friendly and laid back in demeanor. In some ways, the business culture was more like Kansas City than New York.

The Canadian market was about a tenth the size of the United States market in terms of trading volume. That probably wasn't enough to be interesting to our bigger rivals, but for us, if we did it well, it would be enough to move the needle.

What made the Canadian opportunity most interesting was that the Toronto Stock Exchange (the TSX) was for the first time facing a serious challenge from a number of new markets including Alpha, Chi-X, and Pure. For most of its history, the TSX had enjoyed a near monopoly. Overnight, they were facing real competition and needed to adapt quickly to guard their market share.

Andy and I made three trips to Toronto. Other associates joined us on some of these visits. We met pretty much all the major players in the Canadian securities industry. We interviewed all the brokers, learning much about the landscape. We carefully considered who we wanted to partner with and chose CIBC.

We also met with the TSX and its competitors. Having recently stepped away from BATS, I was probably more familiar than anyone on the planet about how you played both offense and defense among markets. All of the market centers were eager to pick my brain. I genuinely told each of them how I would be playing the cards if I was in their position. This was a topic I loved to talk about.

The Third Family Trip
Our family (Jamie, Nicole, Joe, and I) took a trip to Toronto in August 2008. Nicole was 11 and Joe was 8. We saw the Toronto Stock Exchange. We stayed at the Royal York and walked through the underground tunnels connecting many of the downtown buildings. We went to the top of the CN Tower (at 1,815 feet, it is the tallest free-standing structure in the Western Hemisphere). The Canadian National Exposition occurred during our visit, so we got to visit that as well. We rented a car and drove down to the Canadian side of Niagara Falls, having lunch in the revolving restaurant tower. Tradebot was expanding into Canada, and it was important for me to share with my kids what that meant. It was one of our best family trips.

Live Trading in Canada
Tradebot was one of the first serious American high-frequency trading firms to expand into Canada. At the time, most of our competitors were focused on Europe.

On schedule, Tradebot went live in Canada in October 2008. To make a long story short, things went extremely well. Our second month, November 2008, we were the largest HFT participant by volume in Canada with over 10% market share.

With a few adaptations, our US trading models worked very well in the Canadian market. In 2009, Tradebot made just over $20 million trading in Canada. This was well above even our most optimistic predictions. Andy O'Hara was promoted to Vice President of International Trading at Tradebot. Our success in Canada gave Tradebot confidence.

Back to the Futures
'Back to the Futures' was a project we did in 2010. Tradebot had traded futures from 1999 to 2001, and then stopped trading futures when we switched our focus to stocks. Rob Alumbaugh and some of the traders led a project that got us back into futures trading.

We focused our trading on CME futures. As mentioned in part one, the futures market is different from the stock market in several ways. For one, there are no rules against insider trading. Two, the CME essentially has a monopoly on the products it trades. Trading fees are higher than the fees for stocks. The pricing increment between the bid and offer price is also wider.

We tried several trading models. Different traders came up with different ideas, but honestly, none of our futures models were consistently profitable.

After more than two years of trying and some relatively small losses, we decided to shut down our futures trading project.

Trading is a tough business. Even though Tradebot was good at stock trading, we were unable to find much success at futures. Our lack of success humbled us a bit. Someday, we may take another run at it.

Europe

Andy suggested we now consider Europe. He studied the European markets and put together a rough project plan. I began to think about Europe and started asking some tough questions, "If we get into Europe, why do we think we will win?" Like America, Europe has very competitive markets. We ultimately decided to pause the project and not expand into Europe at that time. About once a year, Andy asks me if we should consider Europe. "Maybe next year" is my usual reply.

The Fourth Family Trip

Our fourth family trip was to Europe. Jamie and I traveled to London and Paris. It was the first time she had been across the Atlantic. We did the normal tourist things like visiting Windsor Castle, the Tower of London, the Eiffel Tower, and Notre Dame.

Mark Helmsley runs BATS' European office. He had been asking me to visit them in London for several years. It was a beautiful office in downtown London on the banks of the Thames River. The view was quite amazing. Mark was delighted to give us a tour and introduce us to his team. I'm glad we finally made the trip.

The Golden Age for Electronic Trading

Let's shift the discussion back to the United States. I consider 2007 to 2010 'The Golden Age of Electronic Trading'. Reg NMS was adopted on August 29, 2005 and was phased in through 2007. This new market structure set forth by the SEC was a big improvement for the average investor. The old floor-based monopoly on trading NYSE-listed stocks had finally been broken. Nasdaq and NYSE-listed stocks now basically traded under the same set of rules, except for a few small differences like how the exchanges handled opening and closing auctions.

There were four significant exchange operators in U.S. equities: Nasdaq, NYSE, BATS, and DirectEdge. There was an intense competition between them for market share. All equity markets in the US were allowed to trade any stock listed on any exchange. The competition between markets kept the fees for trading low. It was the best of all possible worlds.

162

DirectEdge had evolved from a small first generation ECN called Attain, which was purchased by Knight. After a couple of management changes, DirectEdge looked nothing like the old Attain. It was run by Bill O'Brien, the former President of the Brut ECN. Basically, DirectEdge had run a similar playbook to BATS, except their investor coalition included Knight, Citadel, UBS, and Goldman Sachs. (Jumping ahead to 2014: BATS completed a merger with DirectEdge on January 31, 2014, reducing the number of significant stock exchange operators from four to three. This reduced competition made me a bit nervous.)

In addition to the exchanges, around 2007 a new breed of market centers began to emerge called 'Darkpools'. The darkpool name was a reference to the fact that, unlike exchanges, darkpools did not distribute quotes. All orders in their systems were hidden or 'dark'. This was done because of the intricacies of Reg NMS that put non-exchanges at a competitive cost disadvantage if they distributed quotes. As a practical matter, as long as we had quotes from the exchanges, we did not really need quotes from the darkpools.

In the space of a couple years, most of the large investment banks each launched their own darkpool. We were quick to work with the banks. I knew firsthand that the key to launching a new trading center was getting a critical mass of liquidity quickly. The banks knew this and reached out to the major high-frequency trading firms like Tradebot, Getco, and Virtu.

Arms Race

Electrification of the markets changed everything. I had imagined in 1999 that algorithms would displace humans for the majority of trading. Now this notion was quickly unfolding across Wall Street.

'Relationships' mattered less in this new world, and technology was the key differentiator. Some of the big banks were woefully behind the HFT firms in their use of technology. We knew we were in the right place at the right time.

The market averaged about four billion shares traded per day in 2004. When Reg NMS was being debated, I told people volume would quickly grow to six billion. Most of the leading firms thought I that was crazy and predicted low double-digit growth. Over time, even my predictions were too low. By 2009, an increase in volatility boosted average daily market volume to 9.76 billion shares per day. Electronic trading was changing everything. Businesses needed to rapidly adapt or die.

The rollout of Reg NMS, followed by the extreme volatility from 2007 to 2010 combined to create amazing opportunities. High-frequency trading was very profitable for a number of firms during this period. Increasing profitability attracted increasingly large investments from private equity firms. Tradebot was not seeking outside capital, but several of our competitors including Virtu and Sun Trading received big private equity investments.

In addition to capital, the HFT industry attracted some of the best technology minds in America. It was an arms race with extremely high stakes. Firms competed to make their systems faster and smarter. The major computer vendors started designing systems specifically for the high-frequency trading industry. There were significant performance improvements around networking and routers. In many ways, aggressive spending by HFT firms drove technology innovation, not just on Wall Street, but throughout the entire computer industry.

Our competitors ramped up their game. Not wanting to be left behind, Tradebot significantly increased our level of technology spending.

The End of the Golden Age

'The Golden Age of Electronic Trading' ended on May 6, 2010. On that day, the market experienced what came to be called the 'Flash Crash'. Public confidence in the markets was severely shaken.

The Dow Jones Industrial Average (the Dow) is the most widely followed stock index. From the previous close, the Dow dropped 998.50 points (about 9%), with the final 600 point dive occurring in less than five minutes. It recovered almost as quickly as it dropped, closing down only 347.80 points.

Why did the market crash so suddenly and then recover so suddenly? The market had good fundamental reasons to be jittery that day. Rumors were circulating that Greece might default on its debt. Against this backdrop, a large mutual fund sold $4 billion of CME stock index futures using an algorithm that was very aggressive. When the futures dropped, the stocks followed. The large sale in futures caused an imbalance between sellers and buyers. When someone trades very aggressively, especially mid-day, you have to wonder if they know something you do not. It is not illegal to trade on inside information in the futures market. Did they know Greece was going to default?

After a few minutes had passed, humans had a chance to check the news and realize that the move was overdone. The markets recovered, as they should have. The thing that was so shocking was how fast the markets had dropped, and then how fast they recovered. As a result of the flash crash, the industry learned an important lesson:

"Markets must be designed to prevent trading at ridiculous prices."

After the market closed, I spoke to my friend, Dan Mathisson, at Credit Suisse. We knew the Flash Crash would be very bad for the industry. We also knew the solution was something called 'Limit Up/Limit Down'. Markets work under normal conditions, but when things get crazy, you need to slow things down so humans have time to digest the breaking news. It took almost four years to be fully implemented, but I was glad to see the Limit Up/Limit Down fix that was made to the market in response to the Flash Crash.

For interested readers, there has been much written about the flash crash. You can find it online. There is much finger pointing, and many in the media have tried to pin the blame on high-frequency trading. After a lengthy study, the Commodity Futures Trading Commission (CFTC) concluded that HFT did not cause the Flash Crash.

Nevertheless, after the Flash Crash, there was a real change in attitude in regards to market regulation. There have been a couple of books written that have played to people's fears. Since the Flash Crash, everyone in the industry has seen significantly increased regulatory costs. This is so unfortunate, because ultimately, these costs are passed along to investors.

Since the Flash Crash, I have done much soul-searching. I am very knowledgeable about market structure. After much pondering, I firmly believe that electronic trading and HFT have been a huge net benefit for the average investor. Spreads have tightened, and the cost of trading has dropped significantly. Electronic markets are not perfect, but they are much fairer and much more efficient than manual floor-based markets. I feel good about what we do. I have learned to accept that the vast majority of the public will never appreciate the role that HFT plays in a healthy market.

15. Investing

In this chapter, I want to share my thoughts about investments.

I was once called 'The worst stockbroker in the world.' Therefore, I do not give investment advice, and I do not manage money for others. However, I will outline an approach that works for me. You can and should make your own decisions.

While I was in college, I opened my account with Charles Schwab. At first, I did not have much to invest. As my resources grew, I added to my account. I still have the same account number that I had in college.

I believe that saving and investing are important. If I had not saved and invested over the years, I never would have had the capital to start my business. I never would have had the down-payment to buy our first house. Many people do not have the self-discipline to save. I once read that over half the country has less than $1,000 in liquid net worth. In a land of so much opportunity, this is completely nuts. There were times in my life when I did not have much income, so I did not spend much. My wife grew up with even less, so she was even more frugal. It is not about income, it is about self-discipline.

My Portfolio

My Schwab account is a standard retail brokerage account. The account is used for investments, not trading. Investing and trading are two very different things. When I invest, my typical holding period is measured in months or years.

At any given time, I usually own a portfolio of about 30 to 100 publicly-traded stocks. Most are large cap stocks in the S&P 500. I try not to invest more than 3% of my net worth into any one public stock. I pick companies that I understand. I buy companies that I am proud to own. I like to patronize the businesses I own. When I shop in a store, eat in a restaurant, or use a product, it makes me happy when I know that I own a piece of the company.

About once every five weeks, I review my account. Obsessing more frequently is counter-productive. When I look over the account, if a stock is down more than 10% from where I bought it, I sell it. I take a tax loss and quit thinking about it. Even if a company is a good company, sometimes my timing is wrong. I do not want to invest in losers. I want to invest in winners.

The nice thing about large-cap public stocks is that they are very liquid. If I ever need money, I can sell a stock. If I no longer believe in a company, I can sell their stock. Real-estate and private equity investments do not have this liquidity advantage.

Over the years, my Schwab account has grown quite substantially, partly because of deposits and partly because of my investment returns.

At the end of each calendar year, I donate my best-performing stock to charity. Donating an appreciated stock, after holding it at least one year, is very tax-efficient. Schwab has a program called the Schwab Charitable Trust that makes this very easy. I just go online and select the stock and the number of shares. It goes into my donor-advised fund. From the fund, I recommend grants to the charities I want to support. It is much easier than trying to give a stock directly to a charity. I once considered setting up a private foundation but realized that using a donor-advised fund involved much less paperwork.

Index Funds

I do not own any actively-managed mutual funds. Sometimes I use low-cost ETFs if I want to invest in commodities like gold or adjust my overall exposure to the market. I am fully capable of picking my own stocks.

Beating the market is hard. In my opinion, the average person would be better off working on something else. Not everyone has the time or interest to pick individual stocks.

For my Roth IRA account, I just buy ticker symbol 'SPY' and forget about it. The beauty in this approach is in its simplicity. I decide how much risk I want, and then buy that amount of SPY. Done.

Why SPY? SPY is the most liquid stock. I will be able to buy and sell it easily whenever I want. It is an exchange traded fund tracking the Standard and Poor's 500 index. With SPY, I will not beat the market, but I will get approximately the average market return. Fees are below a tenth of one-percent per year. Why pay high fees to get an average return?

Is the Market Fair?

After the economic meltdown that started in 2007, it has become quite fashionable to bash Wall Street. Some claim that "the market is rigged". Folks, this is simply not true. The American stock market is the best and most liquid in the world.

Since Reg NMS in 2005, the market has never been more fair for retail investors. Most market structure criticism comes from two groups of people. First are former floor traders. Reg NMS made the markets fully electronic and totally destroyed their little racket. The old floor trader games are never coming back – and that is a very good thing for investors. Second are underperforming asset managers who want to be paid for beating the market, yet routinely deliver crappy results. Face it, losing money for your clients does not make you a market structure expert.

I opened my retail account at Charles Schwab in 1989. In those days, the bid/offer spread was often 25 cents. In 1999, I vividly recall reading on the NYSE website, "We fill the average market order in only 23 seconds!" The good old days were not so good unless you were on the floor of the big board.

Today, the typical market order fills in less than one second. According to Credit Suisse research, "Bid-ask spreads, currently averaging less than 3 basis points for S&P 500 stocks, are at the lowest levels ever. " (Ana Avramovic, May 15, 2013).

When I want to invest in stock, I log into my Schwab account. To get the best fills, I avoid trading on days the market is going crazy. I also find the most liquidity in the last hour of the trading day. I always use limit orders. In most stocks I follow, the bid/offer spread is usually a penny. When I place my order, I often get 'price improved', meaning I get a fill that is even better than the quoted spread. If I place a marketable order, it is usually filled up to the quoted size or more in less than a second. The commission is $6.95. Folks, the market is not broken.

What keeps the market fair?

After studying the market deeply for seventeen years, I have come to realize that it is the competition between brokers and HFT that keeps the market fair.

If you do not like your fill, get a better broker. It is just that simple. Brokerage firms use algorithms to help route and fill customer orders. The top brokers spend millions of dollars developing good technology. They use data to benchmark performance. They constantly improve their systems.

Much of the criticism comes from brokers who have failed to invest in good technology. In fact, if you hear your broker whining about HFT, it is probably an admission they are behind the times. You might want to move your account!

What about Risk?

Investors get upset when the market goes down.

People need to realize that it is impossible to take the risk out of the market. At its most fundamental level, the entire purpose of a stock market is to facilitate the transfer of risk.

In the short run, it is almost impossible to know with more than 55% certainty whether a given stock will go up or down in the next 12 months. Over the very long run, stocks will probably go up if the American economy continues to grow, but in the short term, it is always a crapshoot.

I will let you in on a little secret: investing in stock is risky. It will always be risky. Do not let your brokers' fancy marketing materials convince you otherwise. Some people can tolerate more risk than others. If you cannot handle the risk, reduce the size of your positions. If you are buying stock, you are buying risk. Got it?

Talking to Chuck

I have had my account with Schwab for 27 years. Their service has been good. Yes, there are other brokers out there, but I have always had good luck with Schwab.

Why did I choose Schwab? I felt like Charles Schwab placed the emphasis on educating investors rather than cramming them with useless self-serving recommendations. I wanted to learn about the market and make my own decisions. Charles Schwab's biography sits on my bookshelf.

Schwab started running commercials that featured the tagline 'Talk to Chuck'. So one day, I called my account advisor and asked if I could speak **directly** to Chuck. To my surprise, my advisor was able to arrange a one-on-one meeting with Mr. Schwab.

I flew out to their headquarters in San Francisco. I was nervous. This guy was a hero to me for years, and I was finally getting to meet him in person. They ushered me into his office and we chatted for about an hour. He was very down to earth. We discussed the markets and investor perceptions about the market. What a great conversation.

I concluded the meeting with a question, "You have accomplished so much in business, why are you still at it? What do you have left to do?" He answered, "I just wish more Americans had a brokerage account. As a society, we have to find a way to get more people involved as owners."

As I write this, my bank pays me less than 1% interest. Mr. Schwab was right. More Americans need brokerage accounts. Get your money out of the banks. They are not a good deal.

The worst stock broker in the world and the best stock broker in the world finally got to chat. Thanks, Chuck.

16. Ventures & Adventures

Entrepreneurship is in my blood.

To me, there's just nothing more exciting than taking a blank sheet of paper, writing a business plan, and watching a business be created around an idea.

Each business is its own life form. It's born, grows up, matures, and someday - dies. A few businesses even fork off their own children. It has a heart and a soul. Every day, it learns and evolves. It is greater than the sum of its parts. A healthy business makes a profit. A great business provides a sense of excitement, a sense of adventure, and a sense of purpose for its associates.

Launching a New Business

Before a business launches, its founder should think deeply about what they want to accomplish. Every business is different. There is not one path to success. There are many paths and many definitions of success.

Some days, I just sit and ponder. A good business starts with a good vision. It is much quicker and cheaper to refine your vision before you get too far along. As a business idea forms in my head, I switch into research mode. What other companies are in the space? What do I like and dislike about them? What vendors sell products to the space? Combine ideas from several businesses that you admire. Do not try to boil the ocean. Try to find a profitable niche to build your first beachhead, and then expand into adjacent markets. How much money will it take to validate the concept? How much time? How many people? How many customers? Make small bets and learn quickly. Adapt.

Once I think I have a decent idea, it is time to start writing. I must admit that writing does not come easily for me. Good business writing is not about quantity, it is about quality. Start with a one page summary. Choose your words carefully. What are you doing? How will you get an edge?

Many new business ideas are bad. Most of my ideas die somewhere between the pondering stage and the one-page summary. This is a good thing. Life is too short to work on everything. Allow only your best ideas to proceed.

For both Tradebot and BATS, I developed a thoughtful business plan. In both cases, it took me about a month of deep reflection. Some people will say business plans are unnecessary, but I disagree. Your ideas get better as you put them down on paper. This is the most cost-effective way to raise your chances of success. Sometimes I have launched a business with just a summary, filling in the details as we went along. None of these businesses have been as successful as the ones where I did a thoughtful business plan upfront.

I'm going to be brutally honest here: If your plan does not generate excitement from knowledgeable experienced venture capital investors - keep pondering. You are not ready to launch.

One more thing, not everyone is cut out to be an entrepreneur. Launching a business is extremely risky. It takes a thick skin. There will be many setbacks along the way. You will be told 'no' a thousand times. Frankly, true entrepreneurs are a bit crazy. By our nature, we are unrealistically optimistic about our chance of success.

Two Paths

As I discussed previously, there are two distinct ways to structure your business in regards to capital. There is no middle ground. The two paths are:

1. Start Small and Own it All.
2. Go Big or Go Home.

Start Small and Own it All. Tradebot went down the first path. We had a few small investors early, but I bought them all out by 2002. If you want to do things your own way, try to own 100% of your business. Outside capital always comes with strings attached.

Go Big or Go Home. BATS went down the second path. We raised over

$150 million of professional venture capital in six investment rounds. Every time I raised money, I got diluted. In 2016, I owned roughly 4% of a $3.2 billion dollar business. If you go down this route, you cannot hold on too tight. Give up control of the board. Allow the investors to fire you if they want. Your investors will be focused on their investment return, not helping you create your dream job. These are the rules that big venture capital expects.

No matter how many times they tell you they are 'long-term oriented', realize that professional venture capital is looking for a big exit in three to ten years. If the market capitalization of the business is above a billion, you may be able go public and stay independent. If the value is between $100 million and $1 billion, they will generally try to sell out to a larger business. If you do not realistically expect to build a business that is worth at least $100 million by year ten, you probably should not seek professional venture capital.

Please do not try to seek a middle route between these two paths. It's painful. I know this from experience. Either own it all or let it go. You have to decide. I see too many entrepreneurs hoping to raise money by selling off 10% to 30% of their business without providing investors any meaningful path to liquidity. This is largely a waste of time. It is almost impossible to attract top-tier private equity without giving up control. Based on my experience, you are better off to avoid the middle ground.

Not too many people have founded a billion-dollar business. Very rare are the ones who have founded two or more billion-dollar businesses. BATS passed a billion in shareholder value creation and Tradebot is beyond halfway. Tradebot took longer because I took little outside capital. Both paths are interesting. Don't get stuck in the middle. Pick your path.

Tradebot Ventures

Rob Alumbaugh was the CEO at Tradebot. He ran the day to day operations, leaving me time to focus on my pet projects and investments.

In 2008, I set up Tradebot Ventures to help grow and fund new businesses. The rule of thumb for venture capital investing is listen to 100 pitches, take 10 meetings, and make one investment.

Knowing this, I built a one-page Tradebot Opportunity Template. It's free and available at www.tradebotventures.com. If you are thinking about raising capital, I urge you to fill out the template. Even if you do not seek an investment from us, put together a well-written one-page opportunity template. It will save you and your potential investors a ton of time.

Nine times out of 10, the answer you get will be a quick, "Thanks for showing us the opportunity, but we are going to pass." The tenth time you will get a serious meeting with an investor that has a serious potential interest in your business.

Know this: venture investing, especially early stage investing, is all about the fit between the entrepreneur and the investor. We do not want to make an investment if we cannot add significant value and insight at the board of directors level. Different private equity firms like different size deals, different industries, different cities, different products, and different teams.

There is a saying,

> *"Smart money early, big money follows."*

I know from my BATS experience that this is totally true. I took a lower valuation to get the investors I wanted, and it paid off big-time.

Business Models

So what kinds of businesses do I like? Ones that can scale, of course. I like financial services. I like software. I like real-estate. I like online businesses. I like businesses that can get to scale with less than 100 associates. I like businesses with a high net revenue per associate. I love businesses that are built around great proprietary software. I like businesses headquartered near Kansas City. No business meets all these criteria, but it gives you a general sense of where my interests lie.

What do I not like? Businesses where I don't think I can add value. I just do not have any interest in sectors like biotech or medicine. I do not invest in businesses that I wouldn't be proud to be associated with (i.e. payday loans or marijuana). I'm not saying these industries are not profitable, just that I will not be spending my time on them.

Tradebot Energy

Greg Emory and Andrew Korte sought an investment in their wholesale electricity trading business. They had previously traded electricity for Aquila and knew the industry well. Wholesale electricity in the Midwest is traded on a platform called MISO (Midcontinent Independent System Operator).

Greg and Andrew's approach to the energy markets was largely manual with some spreadsheets to help analyze the data. We hoped to combine their industry knowledge with our ability to build automated trading systems.

Working together, we got an energy trading system up and running. It was a combination of automatic analysis, overlaid with human judgement from Greg and Andrew. For the first six months, the trades we made were a bit better than break even, but things did not scale quite as well as we had hoped. Every now and then, the system would experience losses that erased several days of profits. While manageable, these drawdowns kept us from increasing our risk limits in energy.

At the end of the year, Greg and Andrew decided to go back to trading on their own. Our team also kept trading using some of the strategies we had developed together. Under the agreement we had made with them, we each got to keep a copy of all energy trading software that we had developed together. We parted ways on good terms.

After about a year trading on our own, we decided to exit the electricity trading business. We were still about break even, and had about five associates dedicated to the project.

Things did not quite turn out as well as we had hoped, but it was a good learning experience for Greg, Andrew, and our team.

Scale

Capitalism is messy.

> *"The key to success is to scale the winning bets."*

We cut our loses quickly when things are not on track. We knew at the beginning that early stage investing is risky. I have no regrets about the investments we made. We learned from all of the entrepreneurs we worked with. They are good people.

We still look at early, mid, and late stage venture capital and private equity opportunities. Our failures have made us humble and more selective. We have passed on a couple businesses that have gone on to profitable exits. I do not worry about that. Someone once told me, "There's always another deal."

One learns quite a bit by reading business plans from a variety of industries. When we first started making venture capital investments, we considered everything. At one point, we even had a gold mine in Arizona.

I wish I could report that we made lots of money on our early stage investments, but that is not what happened. We had a handful of other small investments. Each failed to reach scale. We lost money.

Over time, our focus shifted from venture capital to real-estate development investments, which I will describe in the next chapter.

Dave's Family Office

My financial life was getting complicated, so I set up a private family office. Having a family office may seem weird to some readers. If your financial life is as complex as mine, it really becomes a necessity. I own Tradebot and several affiliated companies. I have several private business investments that need to be monitored. Some years, we look at hundreds of potential investment deals. My team helps me with everything including investments, estate planning, taxes, and charitable gifts.

Selected members of the Tradebot team have a dual mandate and also work on my family office matters in addition to their regular duties. Splitting their time between Tradebot work and my family office gives them a good variety of tasks.

I once considered using an outside wealth advisor, but quite frankly, I consider the Tradebot associates much more qualified. We have several Certified Public Accountants at Tradebot. They know me and my personal situation. They know my preferences. They know my family.

Equally important, I know them. I have an extremely high level of trust in my team. They have access to my personal information and my tax records. As accountants, they know what can be shared and what needs to stay private.

Two key players on my family office team are Jennifer Tomlinson and Eric Buer. Both are CPA's. They take their roles quite seriously.

Jennifer Tomlinson joined Tradebot in 2008 after spending the early part of her career with KPMG as a public accountant. In her interview, I asked her what she liked and disliked about her former job. Her response, "I love everything about my job. I just wish it was 50 hours a week instead of 80."

Jennifer has an amazing ability to juggle many responsibilities and stay organized. She has performed several accounting and finance tasks. She became an initial member of Tradebot Ventures team in 2008. In 2012, she also became Tradebot's Head of Human Resources. In 2015, she added the title of Chief Financial Officer to her plate. In addition to her role at Tradebot, Jennifer is also a working mom with two young kids. I have no idea how she makes time for everything.

Eric Buer joined Tradebot in 2009. He had previously worked with Jennifer at KPMG. Eric played middle linebacker for Drake University. He is one of the most competitive people you will meet. He is also one of the most coachable. Like my dad, he grew up in Iowa. He is very ambitious, but he wants to work hard to achieve success. His relentless drive infects the whole team. Eric started in accounting, became Director of Finance in 2010, and Tradebot's CFO from 2012 to 2015. Now, he works mostly on our family office investments. In addition to his formal titles, Eric also plays an amazing number of roles within the firm.

In addition to Jennifer and Eric, other associates take on family office projects from time to time. When a family office project wraps up, they go back to their regular Tradebot duties. It's nice to have this flexibility in staffing.

Jennifer, Eric, and I make a good team. The three of us meet weekly. We talk about Tradebot and our outside investments. Sometimes our conversations drift to a wide range of topics. Eric is the most aggressive, and Jennifer is usually the most cautious. I ask the most questions.

Think Week

Once a year, I take a 'Think Week'. I started this habit in 2009, the year I turned 40. I unplug from my normal responsibilities and travel to somewhere interesting. On think weeks, I spend time pondering my life, my goals, and my priorities.

Each year since college, I have made a list of goals around New Year's. During the first half of my life, my goals were pretty clear. I wanted to get into a career I enjoyed and that also allowed me to make a significant amount of money. I knew I wanted to get married and have two kids. I wanted a decent house in a good neighborhood. Someday, I wanted to own my own business. By age 40, I had largely accomplished these original big goals. What next?

The second half of my life, goals have been harder to define, and that is where Think Week comes in. What's on my bucket list? Over time, this list has evolved and expanded.

One item on my bucket list was to write a book. I first considered writing a book on my first Think Week in 2009. It was a goal that kept getting pushed to the back burner until I finally made time for it this year. Another item on my bucket list was to become a pilot.

Pilot

In 2009, I bought a Cessna and earned my private pilot license.

Growing up, my dad worked for TWA. He was not a pilot, but worked in management. When I was little, I remember getting to walk through the hanger and see the planes on family day.

Getting my pilot license was hard. At age 40, I felt like I was back in college. I studied nights and weekends. I took off early some afternoons for the flying lessons. Within one year, I got my private pilot license, my instrument rating, and my multi-engine rating. Occasionally, you need to take on a hobby that takes you beyond your comfort zone. Since getting my plane, I have visited all fifty states.

Many journeys were interesting. One of the most memorable was a day trip I took with my son to St. Louis. Joe was playing chess with the Kansas City chess club. Since my son was into the game, I started playing again myself. We visited the St. Louis Chess club, which is one of the best in the country. Through a mutual friend, I was able to arrange a meeting with the former World Chess Champion, Gary Kasparov.

Over dinner, I told Mr. Kasparov about how his match with Deep Blue had inspired Tradebot. He found it interesting and pointed out that he had embraced computers when developing his chess strategies. The middle square of my son's chess board is signed by Mr. Kasparov.

The Family Farm

Jamie grew up on a farm in eastern Colorado. Ever since we were married, she has always dreamed about getting a house in the country. So in 2012, we bought a 144 acre farm with a house on it. It is north of Kansas City near a small town called Smithville. Just north of Smithville is a 7,190 acre public lake where we can go wakeboarding. We bought ATVs, a small tractor, and two Gators [utility vehicles] from John Deere. We spend our summers at the farm, and make occasional weekend visits during the school year.

Shock

After the flash crash in 2010, the electronic trading landscape began to change. There was an increase in hostile news coverage that triggered a political push to increase regulation of the industry. Chief Compliance Officer at Tradebot was once a half-time role. The regulatory aspects of running a broker-dealer expanded to require about three people. HFT firms began getting more frequent regulatory inquiries asking for more documentation and data, up to multiple times per month. Crafting responses to an endless stream of regulatory inquires is not fun.

In addition, starting around 2011, market volume and volatility dropped significantly. With so many extremely smart people chasing greatly declining opportunities, the HFT business got much harder. I heard Larry Tabb, an industry expert, estimate that HFT industry profitability in US equities had declined from an annual peak of $5.5 billion to around $1.5 billion. Even if these numbers are not exact, they give you some sense of shrinkage of our industry. The combination of hostile news coverage and declining profitability was not fun.

As we did our year-end reviews for 2011, Rob Alumbaugh shocked me when he told me he had decided to leave the trading industry. He gave us as long as we needed to arrange the transition. It took about eight months, but we managed to move Rob's responsibilities to other people in the firm.

Rob had been with me since the early days. In addition to being our CEO, he had personally coded the most important piece of our trading system, 'the bot'. Beyond work, Rob was also a good friend. I totally understood his reasons, but it was still very hard for me to hear that Rob would be leaving our industry.

Rob is a class act. I appreciate all that he has done for Tradebot.

17. Big Concrete

Somewhere, along my path in life, I learned a very important lesson:

"Only do business with people you trust."

There are several levels of trust. Deeper and deeper levels of trust take years to develop. There are a handful of Tradebot associates who have earned my deepest level of trust and respect. There is also a man named Nathaniel Hagedorn.

NorthPoint

I first met Nathaniel Hagedorn in 2003 when he was a project manager for Briarcliff Development. Charles Garney, Briarcliff's owner, hired Nathaniel straight out of college and had mentored him. Charles and Nathaniel had proven themselves to me twice, first with the BATS office space and then with the new Tradebot office space.

In every business deal, there is the legal contract, and then there is the relationship that stands behind the contract. When the relationship is good, small problems get resolved quickly and fairly. Charles and Nathaniel always went above and beyond the contract to make sure that I was happy as a tenant. Over several years, that is how they have earned my trust.

The Briarcliff team built the office, retail, and housing development where our offices are located. In 2011, Briarcliff Development expanded the project and built an upscale apartment complex on the hill overlooking Kansas City. The project was a hit and filled up quickly.

As the Briarcliff project was nearing completion, Nathaniel and Charles formed a new company, NorthPoint Development, to pursue opportunities beyond Briarcliff. Nathaniel owned the majority of NorthPoint and Charles had a minority stake. Though the two men had great respect for each other, it soon became clear they had a very different tolerance for risk. Nathaniel was full of energy and ready to take on big projects. Charles was now in his eighties and had a much different risk profile.

A deal was reached. Rob Alumbaugh (Tradebot's former CEO) bought out Charles Garney's piece of NorthPoint and became partners with Nathaniel Hagedorn. As you can probably guess, Rob Alumbaugh is a person who has also earned my deepest level of trust.

Tradebot Properties

Tradebot Properties was created to make real-estate development investments. I put Eric Buer in charge. In December 2011, we made our first investment in a NorthPoint project. It was relatively small. Over the next five years, our investments in NorthPoint projects have grown larger and larger.

There was a failed strip-mall project near my house called 'The Tuileries'. The economic downturn was not kind to the project, and it was over 60% vacant. The buildings were well-built, perhaps even over built, but there were design and marketing flaws that caused the project to fail. It was put into bankruptcy. The bank took ownership and put the property up for sale. I saw the sign and called Nathaniel to see if we should make a bid for the property.

As he dug into it, he found out there was not one bank, but three banks with three different loans, all in default, on different parcels of the project. The key to any turnaround would be getting control of all three pieces. I totally forgot about the project after the initial discussion. Nathaniel called me back about a year later saying he finally had gotten all three banks to agree to terms to sell the property. He was looking for investors. We made our first investment in a NorthPoint project.

The property was renamed 'Burlington Creek'. By the way, my wife's hometown is Burlington, Colorado. The NorthPoint team quickly turned around the project. Within a year, the retail space was over 95% leased.

Now, when people ask me what business I am in, I answer:

"Big Data and Big Concrete."

Why Real-Estate?

Every point in the business cycle creates opportunities. From 2009 to 2016, interest rates were at historic low levels. It was a good time to shift our investment focus from venture capital to real-estate development.

In normal times, a person should diversify their investments between stocks and bonds. However, I cannot bring myself to buy fixed income investments at these ridiculously low interest rates. So, I decided to move my fixed income allocation into real estate.

Real estate is a huge sector. Within the sector, I wanted a good rate of return, but I also wanted to fund projects we were proud to own.

Multifamily Apartments

Another motto appropriate for this chapter:

"Charity is not the only way to make the world a better place."

It is great when you can make a for-profit investment that also benefits society. For most families, the cost of their house or apartment is their largest monthly expense, sometimes consuming up to 30% of their disposable income.

An apartment complex behind Burlington Creek was planned. Nathaniel loved the idea that you could walk from the apartments to the retail shops. 'The Residences at Burlington Creek' became another hit project.

Over the next couple years, NorthPoint developed three additional apartment complexes around Kansas City, with each project having around 300 units. Our investment returns were good, but you could also tell that the residents loved the quality of their new apartments. Each complex had retail amenities within walking distance, which was very popular and also good for the environment. There are thousands of small details that go into a good apartment project. NorthPoint got the details right, and each project filled up quickly.

The downtown Kansas City area is in the middle of a major revitalization effort. For many young adults, it is once again 'hip and cool' to live downtown, and downtown nightlife has greatly increased over the past decade as a result. A key part of that revitalization effort is increasing the amount of quality housing within the downtown loop.

The Kansas City Power and Light Building is a 34-story Art Deco office tower that held the title as the tallest building in Missouri from 1931 through 1976. It sat vacant. NorthPoint saw an opportunity to repurpose the structure as upscale apartments. When it reopens, it will once again become the most iconic building in Kansas City. There are many potential projects. It's great when we can make an investment that also has such a positive effect on the revitalization of Kansas City.

Smart Industrial Projects

Beyond the buildings, the best real-estate investments have a strong underlying thesis. One thesis is what I call 'Smart Environmentalism'. In a nutshell, this means reducing the cost of logistics and the impact of logistics on the environment.

Logistics is the transport of goods from their place of manufacture to consumers. Logistics accounts for a high percentage of total fossil fuel consumption. According to the Federal Highway Administration, the average truck consumes 26 times the amount of fuel as the average car per year. If you truly want to reduce global carbon emissions, you have to look at logistics. It doesn't really matter if you drive a Tesla or an SUV. The biggest impact on the environment is reducing the number of truck-miles.

One project we invested in is right outside my window. My office sits on a hilltop overlooking the General Motors Fairfax Assembly plant across the Missouri river. It is one of the most productive plants in the entire GM system. Last year, the plant produced 279,674 cars including the Chevy Malibu and the Buick LaCrosse. As a rule of thumb, one truckload of parts goes into the plant for each car that comes out. What if those trucks could travel a half-mile instead of much further? What impact would that have on the environment? How much money would that save GM and their suppliers?

The United States Federal Government owned the 74 acres next to the Fairfax plant. This overgrown field was once the site of the original Fairfax plant that had been removed in 1986 when they built the new plant next door. (By the way, during World War 2 the site was used to produce the B-25 bomber.)

I decided to buy the land, and we are working with NorthPoint, General Motors, and the GM component suppliers to build a logistics center on the site. It is so much more efficient to build sub-assemblies right next to the plant rather than trucking them across town or across the country. It is a double win when a good investment is also good for the environment. Smart environmentalism.

I proudly drive a American-made Cadillac. It's kind of funny, my first job out of college was working for General Motors. Twenty-six years later, we are building an 800,000 square-foot building next to their plant.

Intermodal

Unfortunately, not everything is made in America anymore. Much of the stuff you buy at the store comes from China. It is shipped to America in sea containers. Last year, the Port of Los Angeles handled 7.9 million twenty-foot equivalent (TEU) containers. Some of that cargo is bound for the Midwest. It could travel 1,559 miles by truck. However, it would be far more efficient, and better for the environment, if it moved by intermodal train. Per gallon of fuel used, a train can move four times as much freight as a truck. Trains are also much safer and have far fewer accidents than trucks.

The Burlington Northern Santa Fe railroad is owned by Berkshire Hathaway. For almost ten years, BNSF was planning to build a massive new rail yard to handle intermodal containers called Logistics Park Kansas City (LPKC). It is on the southwest corner of greater Kansas City in the small town of Edgerton, Kansas. At full build-out, the park will have the capacity to unload 1.5 million intermodal sea containers per year.

Rail yards drive demand for warehouse space. In Edgerton, BNSF had chosen The Allen Group as their development partner. Unfortunately, The Allen Group suffered large losses in the 2008 economic downturn. They no longer had the financial resources to build warehouses around LPKC.

As luck would have it, Patrick Robinson was the project manager for The Allen Group at LPKC. Patrick's roommate in college was Chad Meyer. Chad was the Chief Operating Officer at NorthPoint. Chad is a Civil Engineer and has a background in industrial construction.

In March 2013, NorthPoint put together an investor group to recapitalize the warehouse development around LPKC. The Allen Group rolled their land position into the newly formed Edgerton Land Holding Company (ELHC). Tradebot Properties took the largest stake (52%) in the new entity. There were a handful of other investors in the deal.

With the new capital, ELHC bought up even more land around the rail yard. LPKC is now a 1,500 acre world-class logistics park capable of holding over 17 million square feet of buildings. As of Fall 2016, there are over 6 million square feet built or under construction. One of the things that has made the project so successful was our willingness to aggressively build warehouses on a speculative basis before a lease has been signed. This allows tenants to move in quickly.

The LPKC project is our largest investment to date. NorthPoint has done a great job and attracted tenants like Amazon.com. Dan Tierney from Getco first told me about Amazon in 1999. At a time when Amazon was a scrappy start-up, Dan predicted ecommerce was the wave of the future. Amazon now sells over $100 billion of merchandise per year.

From earlier in this book, you know that I like to see competition between markets. The building right next to Amazon is rented to an online retailing upstart called Jet.com. It will be interesting to see if Jet can compete with Amazon. Jet recently agreed to be acquired by Walmart.

NorthPoint Expands

The culture at NorthPoint is extremely healthy. In a few ways, it reminds me of Tradebot in the early years. Nathaniel and Rob have told me they copied a few elements they liked about Tradebot. I could not be more proud. In other ways, NorthPoint is different from Tradebot, and that is good. Every company has different goals and methods of achieving them.

In less than five years in business, NorthPoint has grown to beyond 100 employees. They have offices in Kansas City and St. Louis. The nature of their business requires some associates to travel extensively. So far, NorthPoint has done amazingly well. They are working on over a billion dollars' worth of construction projects, making them one of the top-ten builders in the country based on square footage under development. Let me remind you, they are only a five-year-old company. It will be interesting to watch their path in the years ahead.

So far, Tradebot Properties has invested in over twenty NorthPoint projects. Some projects have other investors, and some projects are just between NorthPoint and Tradebot. Nathaniel told me that NorthPoint would not have been able to expand as rapidly if it were not for Tradebot investments in NorthPoint projects. So far, we are by far the largest investor in their deals. Yet, to be clear, we do not invest in all NorthPoint projects, only the ones that meet our risk-reward and return criteria. We seek to be value-added as investors.

NorthPoint has earned our trust, and we have increased the size of our investments accordingly. We now have projects in Kansas, Missouri, Indiana, Tennessee, Ohio, Pennsylvania, and Texas, with more in the pipeline.

It is personally fulfilling for me to see NorthPoint succeed. They have the raw talent. They are willing to work hard. They are constantly learning. Yes, they make money, but they go about it the right way and are ethical in all their dealings.

In contrast to public company investments, it is easier to see the impact when I make an investment in a private project. We sometimes walk a jobsite and see over a hundred contractors working, including concrete finishers, plumbers, electricians, roofers, and landscapers. To be honest, I would rather help create jobs than fund charities. Jobs preserve people's dignity and their sense of self-worth. Good, well-paying jobs are what increase the wealth of this nation. I don't know why some people demonize people with capital to invest. The economy will grow if more people make investments.

Pay it Forward

Nathaniel would say he considers me one of his mentors.

'Pay-it-forward' is a cliché often heard in the Kansas City business community. Ewing Kauffman was the founder and late owner of the Kansas City Royals. Kauffman mentored Neal Patterson, the founder and CEO of Cerner. Neal mentored me. I mentored Nathaniel. This year, Nathaniel mentored my daughter Nicole.

Nicole was a senior at Park Hill South High School. As a part of one of her classes, she had to find an internship at a local business. I pushed her hard to apply at NorthPoint. She got the job. Will she learn as much from Nathaniel as I learned from Neal? I have high hopes.

Nicole is off to a good start in the business world. Throughout the semester, she attended several high-level meetings and saw Nathaniel and the other executives in action. With no help from me, she parlayed her unpaid spring semester internship into a paid summer job with NorthPoint. She spent the summer as a leasing agent at the Residences of New Longview, one of the apartment projects I wrote about earlier. She absolutely loves her manager, Pam.

Nicole was so proud of her job, telling me, "Dad, they treat me like an adult. I do the same work that the girls out of college do." Nathaniel once told me that when it comes to business, Nicole is mature well beyond her years. At eighteen, she talks like someone who is at least twenty-five. "Well," I told Nathaniel, "she grew up around a serial entrepreneur."

18. The Tradebot Playbook

We are getting close to the end of the book. I would like to go on another tangent. In this chapter, I want to talk about the culture at Tradebot. Culture is a hard topic to write about, but one that I believe is important.

Every company has a unique culture, a way of doing things that makes them special in some way. I'd like to think we have created a special culture at Tradebot.

Over the years, I have put a lot of thought into how we structure our business. My goal is to build the type of company I would have wanted to work for when I was in my twenties. I believe this design criteria allows us to attract great associates which in turn leads to our success.

I want to build a firm that is as impactful as possible with less than 100 associates. Why 100? In a small organization, everyone knows everyone. In a larger organization, most people only know about 100 people well. Many entrepreneurs have grown their companies to the point where, "It's just not fun anymore." My theory is that you maximize happiness at work by working with less than 100 people that you know and respect.

Everyone at Tradebot works on one floor in one building. Our floor was designed to hold 100 people. We currently have around 65 associates so there is still some room to expand.

Throughout the year, I make a point of eating lunch with everyone in the firm. When we want to have an all-company meeting, everyone fits in the classroom.

Decisions are made quickly. Everyone knows they can drop by my office or catch me in the hall if they have a question. Communication must be harder in a larger organization. I believe our ability to stay nimble is a key competitive advantage.

Over the years, our approach has evolved. Each year, we add or remove a few elements as we learn what works. To be clear, I am not saying that our culture is superior to others, only that it works for us. Here are 16 points I would like to make about Tradebot culture.

1. Associates

First, we call our people 'associates' instead of 'employees'. As mentioned in an earlier chapter, this is a practice I learned from Neal Patterson at Cerner. Everyone we hire could get a job elsewhere. They do not just 'work for' us, **they chose to associate with our firm**. There is a difference.

2. ACE

Aptitude, Character, and Enthusiasm. I believe these are the core traits that make great associates.

I got two-thirds of the ACE idea from Bill Grigsby. Bill was the "Voice of the Chiefs" and the longest-serving sports caster in football. I once heard Grigsby give a speech about *Attitude*, Character, and Enthusiasm. Well, it certainly takes *Attitude* to be a great sports caster, but I believe it takes *Aptitude* to be great in business.

Anyone who met Grigsby loved him. We both lived in Parkville, a small suburb of Kansas City. Beyond his day job, he would emcee a community event called Christmas on the River in Parkville. He passed away in 2011. When I go for a bike ride, I ride down to English Landing Park by the Missouri river around a ball field named Grigsby Field.

3. Recruiting

Where do we find great associates?

We recruit from five state schools in our area: Missouri (Mizzou), Kansas (KU), Missouri Science and Technology (Rolla), Kansas State, and Iowa State. The majority of traders and developers start straight after graduation.

Recruiting for accounting, finance, and compliance is a bit different. In these departments, most associates have a background of one to five years in public accounting.

192

Tradebot is a Midwest firm. The majority of our team is from the Midwest. I would rather hire people from the Midwest than people from the coasts.

The Midwest has a much lower cost of living than the coasts. It's full of hardworking people who enjoy a balance between their work and their family life. I enjoy a ten minute drive to work with little traffic and free parking. I love to visit the big coastal cities occasionally, but I don't want to live there.

4. The Tour
When interview candidates step off the elevator, I like to begin their visit by personally giving them a 10 minute walking tour of our floor.

We stop at each department. I get a chance to share some quick stories about the ways our company is unique. We make a first impression on a candidate, and a candidate makes a first impression on us. Looking into their eyes gives me a sense the level of excitement they either have or do not have about our firm.

I also enjoy giving 'the tour' to first-time visitors and other guests. I am proud of what happens on our floor, and I enjoy the chance to tell the Tradebot story.

5. Hiring Process
I follow the tour with a very frank one-on-one discussion.

I ask a lot of open ended questions. Why did you choose your college and your major? What do you like and dislike about your current job? What are your short and long term financial goals? How do you see your career unfolding over the next five years? What would you like to learn? What other jobs are you considering and why?

After meeting with me, the best candidates move on to meet with three or four other managers. For in-town applicants, we usually do this on a second day. For out-of-towners, we do this the same day to minimize travel.

At the end of the day of interviews, the managers pile into my office. Thumbs up or thumbs down? It takes a unanimous thumbs up to get an offer from us. The bar for hiring is very high. I have learned over the years that 'maybe means no'.

We also do background checks and ask for ACT or SAT test scores. Candidates submit resumes and fill out an application. Within 24 business hours, we make a final decision. Either an offer is made or not. Our goal is to treat all candidates respectfully and always let people know where they stand. Even when we do not make an offer, we want the interview process to be a positive experience.

I have often been asked why I do the tours and the interviews personally instead of delegating it. If the average associate works with me ten years at two thousand hours a year, that equates to 20,000:1 leverage on my time. Getting the right people on board is everything. Nothing I do makes a bigger difference to the firm. Not even close.

6. One-Pagers & Meetings
Tradebot has most meetings on Mondays.

When associates develop an idea, I encourage them to write up a 'one-pager'. Writing a one-pager forces you to think carefully about your idea and how to concisely describe the important concepts to others. Good one-pagers start with a highlighted section at the top that lays out the recommended action or key point. The main section often contains bulleted lists. Sometimes there is a key graph or picture.

At meetings, we mostly review and discuss one-pagers. Most meetings contain 3 to 10 associates, so everyone is involved in the conversation. I try to ask questions that will encourage deeper thought on a topic. If we have a decision to make, we can make it and quickly move on to action.

7. Free Lunch
At Tradebot, we have lunch at 11:00am.

The company buys lunch for all associates, every day. We rotate caterers, and we always have pizza on Fridays. Associates often gather in small informal groups.

On Tuesdays, we have 'Tradebot Lunch Mix.' The food is like other days, but each associate is randomly assigned a table. That way, everyone has a chance to eat with people in the company they may not have talked to for a while. These small things work to create a culture where everyone knows everyone.

In terms of impact, buying associates lunch and non-alcoholic beverages has a high payback. I'm surprised more companies don't buy lunch.

8. Year-end Reviews

Each November, we do year-end reviews at Tradebot.

Every associate starts by filling out a one-page summary. The questions asked in the past have been:

1. What were the highlights of the year?
2. What were some of the low points?
3. What 50% of your time adds the most value to the firm (that you would like to spend more time on)?
4. What 50% can be shrunk to 25% to make room?
5. What do you want to learn in the year ahead?
6. What one question would you like to ask the board?

I fill out my one-pager and share my answers with all associates. It keeps me accountable. Associates discuss their one-pager with their manager. Each associate also meets directly with a member of the board. It is important for us to collect unfiltered feedback from all associates.

9. Base & Bonus

Tradebot uses a 'base & bonus' compensation system.

I firmly believe base salary plus discretionary annual bonus is the best way to structure compensation in a private company like Tradebot. New associates often ask me what they should do to maximize their bonus.

"Do what you would do if you owned the firm."

We guarantee all associates a base salary. Salaries tend to be in line with prevailing wages at other companies around Kansas City. At the end of the year, the board sits down and ranks everyone in the company top to bottom, like an NFL draft. Knowing what we know about each associate, if we had to do it over, who would we hire first? Second? Third? All the way down the line. This ranking is the backdrop that determines how we allocate the bonus pool. We grade on a curve, and it is a very hard curve.

We pay out 100% of bonuses in cash every December. We do not use vesting. By design, there are no golden-handcuffs and no stock options. Professional compensation consultants say this is a stupid structure. I disagree.

Using a pay-as-you-go structure has two objectives. First, if someone is burned out or unhappy, I want them to be free to move on at year-end. Every year, as associates return to work in January, I know they are at Tradebot because they want to be and not because they are stuck in golden-handcuffs. Second, many associates have young families. Having access to the money every year is better than waiting for a big event like an IPO that may or may not ever come.

Companies often claim they want their employees to think like owners. The trouble is, most compensation systems cap the upside. We have no caps. Make money for the firm, and you are making money for your family.

By design, Tradebot is in an industry that is hugely scalable. This means we can make a huge amount of money when we win with a relatively small number of associates. This is not by accident. If you want to attract the top people, you need to be in a highly scalable profession.

10. Live on Your Base
I always tell associates to live on their base salary.

Never think of your bonus as an entitlement. The economy goes through cycles. Some years there is just more opportunity than others. If you get accustomed to living on your base, you can get through the down times without too much financial pain. Most associates are good at saving for a rainy day. Some associates use their bonus for a new car or a special family vacation.

In trading, the game is all about making money. Over time, I have learned that this is the yardstick, not the goal. When you are choosing a career, there is nothing wrong with picking one that can make you rich in 10 years rather than 40.

11. Read Business Books

I have read hundreds of good business books over the years.

From age 20 to age 40, I averaged reading a business book a week. I strongly encourage young professionals to read many business books. No one knows everything. The key to reading is to extract bits and pieces of wisdom from each story.

In order to share my love of reading, we did 'The Tradebot Book Club' in 2008. I picked twelve of my favorite books that I thought were relevant to associates. Each month, Tradebot bought any associate who wanted to participate a copy of the book of the month. At the end of the month, we gathered for drinks and discussed what we had read.

Here was our book list for 2008:

1. **The 7 Habits of Highly Effective People**, by Stephen Covey.
2. **Market Wizards**, by Jack Schwager
3. **Wikinomics**, by Don Tapscott
4. **First, Break All the Rules**, by Marcus Buckingham
5. **Confessions of a Street Addict**, by James Cramer
6. **Business at the Speed of Thought**, by Bill Gates
7. **Crossing the Chasm**, by Geoffrey Moore
8. **Joel on Software**, by Joel Spolsky
9. **The Black Swan**, by Nassim Taleb
10. **Way of the Turtle**, by Curtis Faith
11. **Giving**, by Bill Clinton
12. **Straight from the Gut,** by Jack Welch

12. Intellectually Curious

Tradebot is not for everyone.

Intellectually curious associates tend to love our environment. People who dislike change tend to hate it. Information is shared across the firm. Associates are encouraged to use data to help us make better trading decisions.

We expect a lot from our associates. They tend to be self-managed. They act as if they own the company. Problems are found and solved. Managers coordinate resources, but there is not a lot of micro-managing.

I love working with smart people. It is a big part of what keeps me motivated to come to work. When you have a bunch of thoughtful associates, even the lunch or hallway conversations are interesting.

13. Tradebot Presentations
From time to time, I ask an associate to do a 45 minute presentation to the rest of the company.

They typically use about 20 PowerPoint slides to explain what they are working on and why. The presentation is usually followed by questions and discussion. Some people are naturally better presenters than others, but I have never attended a presentation that was not worth the time spent. Learning to present an idea in front of your peers is a great career development exercise.

14. Wrap-ups
In the early days of the company, we would have a short stand-up meeting on the trade floor every day after the closing bell.

As the company grew, wrap-ups became less frequent and moved to the classroom. The room is packed. Over the years, wrap-ups have been our way to share the milestones and the struggles. We introduce new associates. Once a quarter, I talk about our goals and plans. Occasionally, we have a guest speaker. It is nice to be able to get everyone in one room from time to time.

15. Events
Tradebot hosts a variety of events throughout the year.

Our first company event was a Christmas party. The entire company and their spouses fit around a single table at Figlio's restaurant. Every year since, Tradebot has held a Christmas party, and each year we pick a different venue, never repeating the same place twice. We try to find spaces that are unique to Kansas City.

Company events are a good chance to get to know associates and their families. In addition to Christmas parties, Tradebot has hosted a variety of events including family day at the zoo, bring-your-kid-to-work day, poker night, golf outings, Royals games, and Sporting KC soccer games.

16. Giving Back

I expect all associates to give back to the community.

I never tell associates what they should give to, but I do expect all associates to donate to something they believe in. Charity plays an important role in many associates' lives. You will never have 'enough' until you learn to appreciate the value of giving back.

Some years Tradebot matches all of the charitable contributions of all associates. It is amazing to see all of the activities that our associates are involved with. In several cases, a Tradebot associate is on the board of directors or plays a leadership role in a charity.

Giving is a very personal decision. Some associates give away a very large portion of their income, and I admire and respect their decision. Some associates did not grow up in a family that donates, so it is new to them, and they are just starting to give. I respect that. Hopefully, their gifts will grow as their financial resources grow.

In addition to Tradebot gift matching, my wife and I also support about ten charities that we feel strongly about. For example, I grew up watching PBS, and my wife is now on the board of Kansas City Public Television (KCPT).

This paragraph will probably create some controversy, but I want to include it anyway. For me personally, I believe that tithing 10% to charity each year is 'good enough'. Why not give away more? Shouldn't someone who is rich give everything they do not 'need' to charity? I do not think that is wise, and here is why: First, someone who is successful should not feel guilty about enjoying the fruits of their success, as long as they go about it in the right way. Second, we should be good stewards of the resources God has given us. By investing wisely, we make an impact. As our resources grow, we make a bigger impact. I believe there is something noble in making thoughtful investments. Thoughtful investments benefit society. I do not believe there is anything wrong with having money, as long as you invest it wisely and continue to give back.

19. Keeping the Edge

Out of the first 49 Super Bowl winners, only seven have won the following year. No team has ever won the Super Bowl three years in a row. It is hard to get to the top. It is even harder to stay on top.

The stock market has always been extremely competitive. A trading firm must continually reinvent itself in order to survive.

Industry in Transition

On December 19, 2012, Getco agreed to merge with Knight Capital. The new company, KCG, is nothing like the old Getco. Before the merger, profits at Getco had taken a major tumble from their peak. Separately, Knight had its own pre-merger issue after a software glitch caused a $440 million loss in 30 minutes and nearly bankrupted Knight. Getco co-founders Dan Tierney and Steve Schuler no longer work at KCG. Hearing that Dan and Steve had left the trading industry caused me to reflect. I once looked up to them. I had learned so much from watching the rise of Getco under their leadership.

So, who do we learn from now? Virtu Financial is now the HFT industry leader. They went public in 2015. Virtu was founded by former pit trader and NYMEX Chairman Vinnie Viola. Doug Cifu is their CEO. I consider Vinnie and Doug friends. I first met Vinny in 2003. I have toured their trading floor and they have visited Tradebot. One time I even got Vinnie to speak at a Tradebot wrap-up meeting. They are tough competitors, but they are also nice guys.

According to their public filings, Virtu's business is roughly four times bigger than Tradebot's. I have never once been envious of Virtu or Getco. Every time I meet someone wealthier than me, or more successful than me, I always wonder, "What can I learn from them?"

Eric Boles & Will Bryson

After Rob Alumbaugh decided to transition out, we promoted Eric Boles to become Tradebot's third CEO, effective January 1, 2012. Eric was previously our COO and our Global Head of Trading. Eric was the right person to lead Tradebot through our next stage. Profits stabilized after 2012 and started growing again. The struggle made us tougher.

I remained in my Chairman role, and with Eric running the company, I continued to have time to drill into special projects. Many of the special projects involved upgrading our technology.

We also promoted Will Bryson to become Tradebot's Global Head of Trading. Since joining the firm right out of college in 2004, Will had progressed up through the ranks. Will is very competitive, and he is also very well respected on the trading floor. He knows our trading system inside and out.

NewBot

In 2012, planning for Rob's transition, we did another major rewrite of 'the bot'. My original bot was written in 1999 and I wrote the second bot in 2000 when we started the switch to stocks. Rob wrote the third bot, the 'Rob-bot', in 2002 and kept enhancing it for nine years. Though it had served us well, it was probably past due for an overhaul. Rob's bot was written in Visual Basic. The user interface code was intertwined in the same process with the trading logic, which at times slowed down our system response speed.

NewBot was the name given to the code rewrite. Paul Rose led the NewBot project. Paul joined Tradebot in 2003 and had written much of the order handling system. Paul and Kelly Burkhart were on the team that I took with me to start BATS. Paul wrote the major parts of the BATS matching engine. Paul has an incredible mind for engineering. He left BATS and rejoined Tradebot in 2011.

The rewrite and re-architecture touched many pieces of our system including the quote and the order handling logic. We estimated the re-write would take a year. Thanks to Paul and several other members of the team, NewBot was substantially complete and rolled into production in August 2012, over 3 months ahead of schedule. Those of you that manage software teams know how rare it is for a major software project to be completed before the deadline.

Faster & Smarter

While Eric Boles was CEO, we decided to focus on our core. There was an arms race underway, and we put significant effort into improving our technology. Most of our system improvements fall into two broad categories: 'Faster' or 'Smarter'.

'Faster' refers to the time it takes our trading system to react to new market data. If the market is going up, offers to sell need to be cancelled, and new orders to buy need to be made.

Each HFT firm uses its own logic to decide when to place orders. However, if the market is going up, we are all likely to raise our bids. The firm that reacts the fastest gets the trade it wants.

'Smarter' refers to using 'Big Data' to make better trading decisions. HFT is the perfect application for Big Data. We use open-source software like Hadoop and Spark. We keep acquiring data and it seems like we expand our cluster about once per year. As of 2016, our Hadoop cluster contains about 200 nodes and has over 5 petabytes of storage. A petabyte is equal to a million gigabytes.

We capture terabytes of data each day and every data point is timestamped to the nanosecond. We save both our own orders and the market data. We have written a host of software research tasks that operate across our cluster, slicing and dicing the data in various ways. The analysis and classification of trading data is an endless project, but it is a key aspect of our firm's ability to stay on the lead lap in a highly competitive industry.

For seventeen years, we have pushed new code into production almost every week. Most ideas come from our traders and are written into the software by our developers. We try to keep the turnaround cycle tight. Not every new idea works. If we are going to fail, we want to fail quickly and cheaply.

Auxby Computers

In the quest to get faster, we built our own computers. Sam Kear, one of our Network Analysts, was into computer gaming. He adapted one of the liquid-cooled systems he saw on the internet and hardened the design to handle the demands of trading. We built the first 50 machines by hand. They were faster than anything we could buy from Dell.

Auxby is the name of an affiliated company we set up to make our own high speed computers. So far, Auxby has one customer – Tradebot. We hired a KC-based electronics assembly company to build and service about 200 more machines. We think we have some of the fastest general-purpose computers in the industry. We even went out and met with the engineers at Intel. They were surprised by our approach.

FPGA

Even our high speed computers are not fast enough. There are some physical limitations on how fast you can get a packet of data in and out of a general-purpose computer. In order to make decisions in less than 1,000 nanos (a nano is one-billionth of a second), it was necessary to switch to a technology called Field Programmable Gate Arrays (FPGA).

There are two companies that make most of the FPGAs: Altera and Xilinx. I had actually programmed an early Xilinx FPGA way back in 1988 when I was an electrical engineering intern with Eastman Kodak. Back then the FPGAs had about 4,000 gates. Now they have millions of gates.

The hard part about using an FPGA is that it must be programmed in a very low-level language like Verilog, instead of a high-level language like C++. Writing code for an FPGA might take 100 times the engineering effort as writing the same code in C++. Fortunately, I am not the one who programs the FPGA chips at Tradebot. A couple of our C++ developers quickly became self-taught in FPGA programming. A great engineering team likes to take on new challenges, even if it outside of their area of expertise.

Tatora

The NYSE trading floor has largely become an illusion for television.

Most trading is done elsewhere. The CNBC studio occupies the place on the floor where trading posts used to be. While some say trading floors should close entirely, I believe there is a value in preserving the history and tradition of the NYSE. Every day, millions around the world watch as the opening bell is rung. It is the symbol of American capitalism.

The majority of stock trading now takes place in three data centers in New Jersey. The NYSE data center is in Mahwah, the Nasdaq data Center is in Carteret, and the BATS exchange is in the Equinix data center in Secaucus. The Equinix data center also holds many of the dark pools.

In order to get data quickly between data centers, we built our own wireless communication company called Tatora. Going in, we didn't know anything about wireless network design, but that didn't stop us. Once again, our team rose to the occasion and added a new area of knowledge.

Tatora currently has one customer – Tradebot. Did you know that a signal travels about 30% faster over a wireless link than over a fiber-optic line? When we learned this, we quickly realized our fiber-optic network was becoming obsolete. The difficult part about wireless is you have to put a repeater tower about every five miles. The path between Mahwah and Carteret is about 35 miles. It is challenging to lease tower space along the most direct path.

Tradebot Alumni

The departure of Rob Alumbaugh changed the way I think about my years at Tradebot. I became aware that a healthy business is constantly changing, constantly evolving.

'Tradebot Alumni' is what I now call former Tradebot associates. Think about it. Your university is proud of you and glad you spent a portion of your life there. I think that is the right attitude. Great people step on and off the train each year. Some people will stay with the company for twenty years and others will spend a shorter time and then move on to something else. On a personal front, I always find it hard to say goodbye to a good colleague.

After Rob Alumbaugh left the firm, I launched the 'Tradebot Operating Committee'. We meet once a quarter. Rob is on the committee, as are several members of our current management team. I asked Kevin Prine, another Tradebot Alumni, to join the committee starting in 2016. Having a mix of current and former associates gives us the right high-level perspective to talk about the big-picture issues facing our firm.

Kevin Prine & Outreach International

Kevin Prine is the President and CEO of Outreach International. Outreach improves the lives of vulnerable people around the world by helping them discover economically viable business models. It is truly an incredible life-changing charity. They do not give people handouts, they help people learn how to help themselves. This creates sustainable jobs in the poorest countries around the world. When people learn to help themselves, it preserves their dignity. Their ideas spread to neighboring villages. Everything is done by the locals in the local context. Their success is viral.

The Experience

Eric was our CEO from January 2012 until June 2014. He 'retired' at the age of 42. Eric has a very strong Christian faith. He is not driven by what the world thinks, but rather what he believes is right. Eric decided he had made enough money, and wanted to spend more time with this family. The trading business tends to attract people driven by money. Eric was not.

I learned a lot about the world in my discussions with Eric. One time, he invited me to join him and his pastor Reggie at a church conference at Willow Creek. What an inspirational trip. "It is not about the money, it is about the experience", Eric would often say.

CEO Again

They say you never get to go backwards in life. Steve Jobs famously returned to Apple, but it was a very different firm than the company he left. He made it the most valuable company on the stock market by introducing the iPod and iPhone.

I am no Steve Jobs, but I have had the rather rare opportunity to return to a company that I founded. Retaking the Tradebot CEO job at 45, I am a much different person than when I first launched the company at age 29.

Reflecting on my career, I feel like I have transitioned from player to coach. I was once a great software developer. Now, I must admit, there are several guys on the floor that can code circles around me. Even though I do not code much anymore, I am still a technology guy at heart. I believe this gives me a certain credibility with my team.

Once upon a time, I was also a good trader. I rarely trade myself anymore. Yet, my understanding of key trading concepts allows me to ask good questions. Over the past seventeen years, I have worked in or managed virtually every department within the company. My joy at work now comes not from doing things myself, but from helping my team find ways to win.

As Chairman, I once joked that my only responsibility was to have four board meeting a year. Everything else I did because I enjoyed it.

The job of CEO is a much bigger responsibility. At the end of the day, the CEO is responsible for the success or failure of the organization. There is no way I could do the job without a great team. Honestly, I am now more confident in my team than I am in my own individual abilities.

My job is my hobby. Maybe someday my attitude will change, but for now, I do not ever plan to retire. Each weekday morning, I take a walk around the floor. There is nowhere I would rather be. I love working with smart people in the field of technology and finance. I am a serial entrepreneur and that is just the way I am wired.

Reinventing Ourselves

In the trading space, nothing lasts forever. For a firm to remain competitive, it must continue to reinvent itself. I do not like it when we lose good associates, but I have come to accept that about 10% annual turnover is healthy, and perhaps even necessary for growth.

In 2016, Rich Stigall decided to 'retire'. As the last member of the 'axis of innovation', I was sad to see him go and thankful for all he had contributed. However, there is good depth in the Tradebot organization, and every hole creates opportunities for the next generation of leaders to step up. To win, every year we need to field a team of associates that are aggressive and hungry to succeed.

For some people, once they have made enough money, they no longer enjoy the fight. If that is the case, they are better off to step off the field. I saw that with Rob Alumbaugh, Rich Stigall, and Eric Boles. Each of them made the decision to quit trading and walk away from the money. I respect them for making that decision.

Not all turnover is voluntary. Every year I have to cut a few teammates, and that is always the worst part of my job. Yet, some turnover is necessary for growth. We must make room for new talent to join the organization. In my heart, I truly want every departing associate to find a place where they can be happy. I believe deep down that this is best in the long run, but it still pains me when I have to break the news to someone that it is time for them to depart.

While writing this book, I asked Human Resources to compile a list of all the associates who have ever worked at Tradebot. I read each name and smiled. The vast majority of the people I was happy to have known, happy to have hired, and happy to have shared some time with. Maybe a few are reading this book.

One person on that list will not be reading this book. Sadly, Derrick Buttron passed away in 2015 after a long fight against cancer. He worked at Tradebot in the early days. I grew up with Derrick and we went to the same church. We went through Boy Scouts together, becoming Eagle Scouts at the same ceremony. Derrick's passing was a reminder that we never know how much time we have on this Earth. He was a year younger than me.

Running its Course
Sometimes the CEO needs to make a difficult decision.

Our Canadian profit peaked in 2009 and then started to slowly decline. In addition to the increased competition, there were some structural changes which lessened our appetite for the Canadian market. The TSX group purchased Alpha, eliminating a major competitor. Without this competition, the whole Canadian market became less innovative.

In 2016, after a good eight-year run, Tradebot decided to shut down our Canadian trading operation. When we pulled the plug, our Canadian trading operation was profitable, but not profitable enough to justify the amount of labor or capital required.

Before deciding to shut down Canada, Andy O'Hara and the other trading managers discussed the situation in my office. I believe we got into Canada at the right time, and we got out of Canada at the right time. No business opportunity will last forever. I told the team, "Remember the excitement we had when we got into this project. We made good money while it lasted. Do not let the shutdown dampen your enthusiasm for the next opportunity."

The trading space is extremely competitive. Even for a firm like Tradebot, it is hard to make money in new markets. In this book, I wanted to share our successes, but also some of our struggles. The path is not easy. There are pockets of fortune, but potholes as well.

I have been through enough ups and downs to know that this industry goes through cycles. You need to calibrate your expectations. You need to live on your base so you can get through the hard times. Eventually, the wind starts blowing the other direction. By working hard in the difficult years, you position yourself for the next windfall in the cycle. For over seventeen years, knock on wood, Tradebot has not had a losing month, but some years have been better than others.

What's the Next Level?

Many people have asked me, "What's your next level?" Honestly, I don't know the answer, but I keep pondering the question.

In management theory, the Peter Principle states, "Managers rise to their level of incompetence, and then stop." I would like to think that I have intentionally stopped one level below my ceiling. I am at peace with my place in this world. I have met other executives, many of them very successful, who have never gotten to this peace. How unfortunate.

With less than 100 associates, Tradebot is within my level of competence. I doubt if I would enjoy running a larger firm. What is the point of getting big just for the sake of being big?

I continue to ponder new opportunities. As I've aged, I've gotten a bit more humble, and wisdom has caused me to be more selective. Someday, we may find an additional mountain worth climbing, but for now, I like the challenge of the current hill.

Family Trip Five

As I was working on this book, my son Joe and I took a trip to visit NYC. While in New York, we visited the Statue of Liberty and took a double-deck bus tour. Joe remembered the first time he had come to New York and had ridden the bus. In ten years, he has grown so much.

The highlight of my trip was taking Joe down to see the floor of the New York Stock Exchange. Over the years, I've become friends with CNBC reporter, Bob Pisani. He gave us a behind-the-scenes tour of the New York Stock Exchange. We watched Bob and the CNBC team produce their broadcast live from the trading floor. After filming, Bob spoke with Joe, telling him his life story about how he was a real-estate developer in Philadelphia and then had the opportunity to join CNBC. Bob told Joe that you need to find your passion in life. I agree.

After we left the NYSE, Joe and I headed south on Broad. Though the business is long gone, I noticed the old concrete 'Island' sign is still on the building at 50 Broad. We ate lunch across the street, and I fondly told Joe about how I used to trade on Island.

Joe and I also drove down to Six Flags Great Adventure in New Jersey and rode the roller-coasters. As our car ascended the hill, I remembered the time my Grandpa and Grandma had taken our family to Worlds of Fun.

World Record Holders

Not all of the technology developed by Tradebot associates is used for trading. Mostly on nights and weekends over a span of about three months, two of our engineers, Jay Flatland and Paul Rose, built a robot that can quickly solve a Rubik's cube. Each day at lunch they would describe their approach and some of the other engineers would ask questions or make suggestions.

A representative from The Guinness Book of World Records visited

Tradebot on February 5, 2016. Jay and Paul's contraption solved a Rubik's cube in 0.900 seconds, officially breaking the Guinness World Record! News teams covered the event. We invited local robotics clubs.

As I am writing this, I noticed their video on YouTube has over 8.1 million views. You can find it if you Google "World's Fastest Rubik's Cube Solving Robot". Check it out. I was so proud to see Jay and Paul break the record.

What does this have to do with trading? Nothing and everything. I like to hang out with smart people. While there is no direct link, Jay and Paul represent exactly the type of people who like to work at a place like Tradebot. We get our edge through great engineering. They would rather spend their free time working on a Rubik's cube robot than watching sports. Engineers may never run the fastest or jump the highest, but two guys on our team broke a Guinness World Record! How cool is that?

Concerned Care Update
In 2016, Concerned Care merged with a similar business. They renamed the combined entity 'Life Unlimited'. As I said, BATS went public in 2016. I took some of my BATS stock and gave it to Life Unlimited so they could buy several new houses for their developmentally disabled residents.

There is a passage in the Bible where Jesus implores us 'to help the least among us'. When I hear that, I think about the residents of Concerned Care and Life Unlimited. I met with their leadership before giving them the gift and I told them, "Sometimes God needs two hands." My hand makes money, and your hand touches people's lives.

I think it was more than a coincidence that Tradebot was located upstairs from Concerned Care.

BATS Update
As I was writing this book, the Chicago Board of Options Exchange (CBOE) offered to acquire BATS for $3.2 billion, pending shareholder and regulatory approval. Eleven years ago, BATS was just a blank sheet of paper on my desk. Now, it is a key part of the American trading

landscape. Whatever path they take, I hope BATS always remembers to keep the customer first. That is the primary reason they were successful.

I went far beyond my comfort zone, I learned a ton, and met lots of very talented people. A few times, I got in way over my head, but somehow it all worked out. Launching BATS transformed my career, yet for me, my time at Tradebot has always been the most enjoyable.

Wall Street

I've always thought of myself as an outsider on Wall Street.

Before you get to know people in the business, it's easy to think of Wall Street as one big evil machine that takes advantage of the little guy. In reality, it's more of a complex interwoven network comprised of some of the smartest people in the world. Most are trying to get rich. If you can make a buck together, they don't care where you are from or what your skin color is, they just want to make money.

The meltdown of the markets from 2007 to 2009 caused the public to hate much of Wall Street. This is unfortunate. We import stuff from all over the world. I often wonder how much of the money that leaves America is repatriated by Wall Street in one way or another. Our standard of living would not be the same without this uniquely American enterprise.

Wall Street is constantly reinventing itself. That is what gives it its power. I recently had lunch at the Majestic Deli. It sits right across the street from the old Lehman Brothers headquarters. Looking out the window, I see the Lehman sign is gone and there is a new name on the building. Traders are still busily scurrying in and out. The game goes on. The names and the faces change. Most of the people on Wall Street are honest. They are just playing a big game and trying to make money.

There are four games I have come to love: Chess, Monopoly, Risk, and Trading.

20. Conclusion

Looking back, the last seventeen years of my journey have been interesting. Since I started Tradebot in a spare bedroom, my life has gone by quickly. That teenager that I saw when I looked out the window is all grown-up now. Once called Katy Barth, she is now almost 30, is married, and goes by Kate Moore. She is one of the first people with whom I shared my dream about building a 'Trading Robot'. After getting a degree in Finance, she joined Tradebot. She is now one of our best traders. I hope that someday my daughter grows up to be a successful and confident woman like Kate.

Like Bob Pisani discussed, I hope my son Joe finds his passion. I hope that one day he will build his own business. Maybe he can hire a few of his hardworking friends.

I have lived the American Dream as I understood it. As an outsider with a small stake, I managed to find a way to build a business. I raised a family. Most of the time, I was home for dinner by six o'clock. The journey has been enjoyable. I hope my story will inspire others to start their own business.

I have enough. I realize that money is just the yardstick, no longer my goal. Money brings opportunity and opportunity creates more choices. I have tried to live a life that was thoughtful.

There is a verse in the Bible that haunts me, "To whom much is given, much is also expected." I know there is a God. My goal is to understand my role in the greater good. Our time on this earth is short, and for a few days, I have been entrusted with some valuable resources. Maybe someday I will have the wisdom to see where they can best be applied.

Both of my parents are still alive. I enjoyed reading the books they wrote, and I hope they will enjoy reading mine. My kids are on their own journey in life. Maybe one day, they will each write their own book. I hope that I live long enough to read those books someday.

To my family, thank you for sharing so many good memories. Thank you for your support along the way. Jamie, I know it is not easy to live with an entrepreneur. As you know, we are wired a bit differently than normal people.

To my associates, thank you for working with me. We have found ways to win, and we should be proud. There were times when I was not easy to work with, and I appreciate your understanding. Hopefully, I have earned your respect. You have earned mine.

Our offices sit on a hilltop overlooking Kansas City. Highway 169 passes by our office. Thirteen miles north up the highway lies our family farm in Smithville. Continuing north, the road bends west and then back to the east, before continuing north again. Following the windy road for 76 more miles, one passes by the original Sager Brothers' Garage in Stanberry, Missouri. Like Highway 169, my path has not always been straight, it has taken a number of twists and turns. The scenery was interesting, and there were many good people to meet along the way. Along my journey, there were many good laughs and a few bitter words that I have long-ago forgotten. In this book, I have shared "the best part of my day," and that is what I intend to remember.

Looking ahead along my path, I wonder what the next seventeen years will bring? Maybe someday, I'll have to write another book…

Feedback?

This story has been building up inside of me for several years. Thank you for letting me share it with you. I would greatly appreciate your feedback: *feedback@makethetradebook.com*

Acknowledgements

Dave Cummings wrote this book and is solely responsible for its content.

Thanks to Jennifer Tomlinson and Alyx Hubler for looking over my drafts and offering feedback. Before release, the book was shared with a small group including Eric Buer, Ryan Albarelli, Scott Ramon, Clayton Harper, Kelly Burkhart, Will Bryson, Andy O'Hara, Daniel Krejci, Rush Olney, Paul Rose, Kate Moore, Nathaniel Hagedorn, Rob Alumbaugh, Kevin Prine, Ken Conklin, and my wife, Jamie Cummings. Thank you for your feedback and suggestions.

Without support from my family and the hard work of my associates, this journey never would have been possible. There have been so many enjoyable memories. Thank you from the bottom of my heart.

Finally, thanks to the many people I have met both on Wall Street and around Kansas City. The friendships made are what have made the journey worthwhile.

About the Author

Dave Cummings is the owner and CEO of Tradebot Systems. Once called, "The Worst Stockbroker in the World", he built a very successful electronic trading business.

Dave is a serial entrepreneur and has launched several businesses including Tradebot Ventures and Tradebot Properties. An engineer at heart, he holds a degree in Computer and Electrical Engineering from Purdue University. He lives in Parkville, Missouri, a suburb of Kansas City, with his wife and family.

Dave is also the founder and former CEO of BATS Global Markets. Launched in 2005, BATS became the second largest stock market operator by volume in America.